The Sword

The Sword

*The Blessing of Righteous
Government and the Overthrow
of Tyrants*

Randall A. Terry

The Reformer Library
Windsor, New York

To David Drye
A Righteous Warrior of Truth
A True Elder in the Gates

CONTENTS

Author's Note

The Sword was written in federal prison in January 1995. Portions of this text will refer to instances and leaders from the time known as the Reformation. This book does not deal with the excesses of Protestants or Catholics during this era. (Let another brave soul tackle that!) Instead it deals simply with the theology of submission to righteous civil authority and the overthrow of tyrants that is part of both Roman Catholic and Protestant theology. The American reader will thus see the critical place this theology played in our own birth as a nation.

If you have any thoughts, feel free to write me at this address:

P.O. Box 570
Windsor, New York 13865

PART ONE

The Divine Origin
of the Sword

1

God's Law
Without Apology

Why do we have government?
Why should we submit to civil government?
Is it ever appropriate to seek the overthrow of a government by the use of force?

I write in hopes of giving concise, Biblical answers to these and other questions. The main body of thought will revolve around two issues:

1) The Biblical purpose for civil rulers, and

2) The Biblical foundation for revolution against civil rulers.

Although some may insist that these are contradictory principles, they are not. Godly obedience to or righteous rebellion against civil authority spring from one root: the Sovereign Kingship, the Unchallengeable Authority, and the immutable Law of God.

The rule of Christ is the fount from which flows the authority for righteous civil authority to govern as well as the authority to overthrow wicked despots.

Herein lies no new theology. This was the theology that animated John Knox and the Scottish reformers in their uprising against Mary Queen of Scots; this was the theology that undergirded Oliver Cromwell in the Puritan revolution against and the final execution of Charles I; this was the theology that ended the monstrous repressive doctrine known as "the divine rights of kings."

Tragically, most Christians today have no idea how critical that history and its attendant theology are to them personally. Most Christians in America at the changing of this millennium do not have a clue who John Knox or Mary Stuart or Oliver Cromwell or Charles I were. Most of us are the victims of the dumbed-down government schools which deliberately ignore Christianity's indispensable link with our history. It is no surprise that most Christians would know little or nothing of the great theological battles that were waged and the critical theological truths that catapulted men and nations into conflict and even revolution.

However, what nearly all American Christians do know is that the birthday of America is celebrated on the Fourth of July. Most also know that that day also celebrates the signing of the Declaration of Independence, which called for revolution against King George III.

If pressed as to why the colonists revolted, some might blurt out "taxation without representation" and end there, hoping not to be embarrassed but intuitively knowing that far more had to be at stake. In fact, the Declaration of Independence gave an extensive line upon line indictment of the atrocities of George III which marked him as a tyrant. While it is true that taxation without representation was listed in the declaration (in different words) as one of King George's offenses against the colonists, it simply was not the mainspring for the revolution, and it obviously was not the *guiding principle* that led the founding fathers and the revolutionaries to call for the overthrow of a tyrant. The undergirding principle of the Revolution was that God had endowed men with unalienable rights—life, liberty, and property—and that it was the duty of government to protect those rights. Subsequently, the state or the king could not arbitrarily violate any of these three fundamental, God-given rights. If the state *did* flagrantly violate these rights—rather than abide by its God-ordained mandate to protect life, liberty, and property—the people could overthrow the government.

But more importantly, the Declaration spelled out clearly the *authority* by which the citizens could revolt against a tyrant: the authority of God and His Law. The founders believed that God and His Law authorized them to break the yoke of George III from their neck. "No king but Jesus" and "Rebellion to tyrants is obedience to God" were both common phrases during that historic era. Our forefathers' explicit belief that God had authorized them in His Word to overthrow tyrants *sprang from the same root of theology that fed the Knoxian and Cromwellian revolutions.*

The names of Knox and Cromwell were more common to America's founders than the founders' names are to us. And the glorious Christian theology that Cromwell and Knox lived out—that God is King and His Law is supreme—gave inspiration to birth the greatest nation that the world has seen since ancient Israel.

Not only did the founders find the undergirding for revolution in Christian theology, they also found the *principles for governing.* Yes, Christian theology provided the fire for revolution, but more importantly, Christian theology was their *foundation for governing.* With virtually unanimous voice, the founders and leaders of America for its first one hundred years believed that Mosaic Law and Christian principles (also referred to in part as natural law) were the bedrock upon which this republic was and must be built. This theology helped make America great politically and socially. Abandoning it has helped destroy us.

For the unbeliever who reads this with a haughty, jaundiced eye, I say this: I gladly confess that I want to see civic law in America (and every nation) restored to and based on the Law given by God to Moses on Mount Sinai and sealed by Christ. I proudly herald the ethical and legal system of Christ and Moses as flawless, infallible and unimprovable—the very best we could possibly build on.

Consider this: at the time Moses received the Law of God, no other nation in the world possessed or practiced a law with such protection of individuals, such incredible land and chattel property rights, such decentralizing of power and authority, such constraints on the power of kings and judges, such rights for those accused of a crime, such just punishment of criminals and compensation of victims. Later, at the time of the resurrection of Christ and the birth of Christianity, almost every nation practiced *human sacrifice*. The spread of Christianity and Christian government alone obliterated that hideous, pagan practice. (By the way, human sacrifice was and perhaps still is practiced *in this century* in India and certain African nations, nations yet unsubmitted to Christ.) It was the spread of Christianity and Biblical law expounded on by Locke and Blackstone and cleaved to by Patrick Henry and George Washington that gave all Americans the political freedoms we take for granted. Yes, I gladly, proudly proclaim that on this Biblical foundation I would see civic law rest.

So now I ask the arrogant unbeliever: upon whose ethical system do you base your standards for civic law? Whose philosophy will you have undergird your vision of American jurisprudence? Would you have the "prophet" Friedrich Nietzsche and his champion, Adolf Hitler? Or perhaps Karl Marx, who expostulated on the glories of equality (the loss of private property) and his murderous disciple Vladimir Lenin, who built Marx's utopia with the blood of millions? Or would you sell us the bloody, chaotic French Revolution and its heroes such as the whoremonger Rousseau, who left his children to die in orphanages, and Robespierre, who helped shed the blood of thousands of innocents? Or perhaps Plato or Socrates, who lived in a culture that practiced human sacrifice and glorified pedophilia?

What religious system would you like to see undergird our culture and law? Hinduism with its oppression of women, child-temple prostitution and degrading caste system? Mohammedanism with its political and religious oppression? How about the atheism of the French Revolution with all its misery, rapine, and bloodshed? Or perhaps would you like to sell us on the new age superstitions and witchcrafts that still keep much of Africa in social and political chaos? Or maybe do you prefer the model of law and order and centralized bureaucracy of Maoist Communist China which mandates forced abortions, shoots its protesting students, jails its Christians, uses slave labor camps, and can't feed its peoples?

Or perhaps would you simply have us submit our political heart and soul to our oligarchical masters—the Supreme Court? Certainly they can create law out of thin air. Or perhaps you would just base society on the innate goodness of man and human reason—the "goodness" and "reason" that has made this the bloodiest, most murderous century since the birth of Christ.

I await your pathetic, liberal arts collegiate answer.

The arrogant, self-assured elitist who dismisses Mosaic Law as archaic, unjust, too libertarian, or too severe has little or no knowledge of history. More importantly, *he or she has absolutely nothing of any relevance to offer in Christianity's place.* They have *nothing* that has been time proven such as the Scriptures. They are bankrupt. Their meaningless philosophies have proven to be *complete failures.* Professing themselves to be wise, they have become fools.

Those who bow down to philosophical idols should be ashamed; believers in Christ should not be. It is the unbeliever's ethically empty emperor who has no clothes.

While the adversaries of Mosaic Law and Christian liberty may not be able to defend their ethics, frankly, they have no need to. They have the reigns of authority. Their naked, embarrassing, drunken emperor is still enthroned. They have captured our courts, our universities, the media, the medicines, and more. American paganism's elite are marching forward with their agenda, and the fruit of their ethic-less endeavors is horrifying to behold. Violence is flourishing, injustice is common in our courts, families are being decimated, youth are filling our prisons, true land ownership is a forgotten memory of the past, and individual rights and freedom—as defined by God—are being crushed before our eyes. Where and how it will end, barring a miracle of grace, we do not know, but we know it must end in death— cultural and societal death—for God has decreed it.

How did we go from the pinnacle of Christian liberty to a cesspool of iniquity and slavery? Many reasons could be cited, all critical in the equation— such as cowardice and corruption in the church, the failure of Christians to be salt and light, a pastorate content to withdraw from cultural conflict and "wait till Jesus comes," theology that predicts defeat and hence becomes self-fulfilling. But I want to focus on one prime first cause, one key reason for America's cultural, economic, religious, judicial, and urban demise: *evil civil magistrates*. Evil rulers, those who abandon God's Law as it relates to civic law, are a prime cause in the moral disintegration of America.

The Proverb declares, "When the righteous are in authority, the people rejoice: but when the wicked beareth rule, the people mourn" (29:2).

God's Word has much to say on government. His Word explains to us:

1. The origin of civil government
2. The purpose for civil government
3. The means of attaining the purpose for civil government
4. The authority *over* civil government
5. The standard for civil government
6. What happens when civil government rebels against heavenly Authority and Law
7. The ultimate means God has given people for removing wicked civil government.

These Biblical principles and theology were commonly known among *average Christians* a century and a half ago. Today we are hard pressed to find one *clergy* in ten who can eloquently expound these themes. The average Christian is clueless.

As the subtitle suggests, *Submission to Civil Authority, and the Overthrow of Tyrants* will observe two opposite sides in this matter: submission and revolution.

Chapter 2 will begin by quoting the most often referenced passage on civil government in America today—which is also the most often abused, misquoted, and taken out of context passage as well—Romans 13. Then the most often cited Old Testament passage in the New Testament, Psalm 110, will follow. Several other passages will then show Christ's unarguable authority over all the governments of men.

Chapters 3 and 4 contain the main thesis. Rather than discuss this in expository form, I have utilized a catechism form—with a question and then an answer. You will recognize many of the questions as your own or ones that you have heard others ask. In my answers I will often reference one of the Bible passages from chapter 2. If I refer to others, I will cite the reference for study. In this manner I hope to provoke the reader to think biblically; if anyone thinks me in error, the response would be to show me how *biblically*.

Finally, several historical documents appear in the Appendix to show the use of the sword in the overthrow of tyrants. These include Patrick Henry's "Give Me Liberty" speech; John Knox's confrontation of Mary Queen of Scots at Hollyrood; Oliver Cromwell's death warrant for Charles I; the United States' Declaration of Independence; Portions of *Lex, Rex, or The Law and The Prince,*; and *Theodore Beza's Right of Magistrates.*

I want to end this first chapter with a disclaimer and then an invitation. First, I heartily admit that this work is incomplete; far from an end-all on this topic, it is at best a starting point. I am hopeful that as such it will provoke further reading, discussion, and thought along the lines proposed. If I am successful in that end, I will be thankful to God.

Second, I invite my brethren—fellow students of the Scriptures, students of history, lovers of liberty—to improve on this work. Perhaps a few men will see a light shining through this darkened glass and will write a more clear rendition of the truths at hand. Should such works emerge as a result of my halting efforts, I shall be eternally grateful to Almighty God.

Finally, it is my hope and prayer that my feeble attempts will give you (by God's grace) a more fervent love for Christ, a greater awe of His Law, and an unshakable faith in and knowledge of His glorious, eternal reign.

Soli Deo Gloria.

2

CHRIST RULES NOW

ROMANS 13:1-6

Let every soul be subject unto the higher powers. For there is no power but of God: the powers that be are ordained of God. Whosoever therefore resisteth the power, resisteth the ordinance of God: and they that resist shall receive to themselves damnation. For rulers are not a terror to good works, but to the evil. Wilt thou then not be afraid of the power? do that which is good, and thou shalt have praise of the same: for he is the minister of God to thee for good. But if thou do that which is evil, be afraid; For he beareth not the sword in vain: for he is the minister of God, a revenger to *execute* wrath upon him that doeth evil. Wherefore *ye* must needs be subject, not only for wrath, but also for conscience' sake. For, for this cause pay ye tribute also: for they are God's ministers, attending continually upon this very thing.

PSALM 110

The LORD said unto my Lord, sit thou at my right hand, until I make thine enemies thy footstool. The LORD shall send the rod of thy strength out of Zion: rule thou in the midst of thine enemies. Thy people *shall be* willing in the day of thy power, in the beauties of holiness from the womb of the morning: thou hast the dew of thy youth. The LORD hath sworn, and will not repent, Thou *art* a priest for ever after the order of Melchizedek. The LORD at thy right hand shall strike through kings in the day of his wrath. He shall judge among the heathen, he shall fill *the places* with the dead bodies; he shall wound the heads over many countries. He shall drink of the brook in the way: therefore shall he lift up the head.

PSALM 2

Why do the heathen rage, and the people imagine a vain thing? The kings of the earth set themselves, and the rulers take counsel together, against the LORD, and against his Anointed, *saying*, Let us break their bands asunder, and cast away their cords from us. He that sitteth in the heavens shall laugh: the

LORD shall have them in derision. Then shall he speak unto them in his wrath, and vex them in his sore displeasure. Yet have I set my king upon my holy hill of Zion. I will declare the decree: the LORD hath said unto me, Thou *art* my Son; this day have I begotten thee. Ask of me, and I shall give *thee* the heathen *for* thine inheritance, and the uttermost parts of the earth for *thy* possession. Thou shalt break them with a rod of iron; thou shalt dash them in pieces like a potter's vessel. Be wise now therefore, O ye kings: be instructed, ye judges of the earth. Serve the LORD with fear, and rejoice with trembling. Kiss the Son, lest he be angry, and ye perish *from* the way, when his wrath is kindled but a little. Blessed *are* all they that put their trust in him.

MATTHEW 28:18-20

And Jesus came and spake unto them, saying, All power is given unto me in heaven and in earth. Go ye therefore, and teach all nations, baptizing them in the name of the Father, and of the Son, and of the Holy Ghost: teaching them to observe all things whatsoever I have commanded you: and, lo, I am with you alway, *even* unto the end of the world. Amen.

COLOSSIANS 1:16–17

For by him were all things created, that are in heaven, and that are in earth, visible and in-

visible, whether *they* be thrones, or domin-
ions, or principalities, or powers: all things
were created by him, and for him: and he is
before all things, and by him all things consist:

COLOSSIANS 2:10

And ye are complete in him, which is the head
of all principality and power.

1 PETER 3:22

[Jesus Christ] who is gone into heaven, and is
on the right hand of God; angels and authorities and powers being made subject unto him.

EPHESIANS 1:18-23 (PAUL, PRAYING THAT. . .)

The eyes of your understanding being en-
lightened; that ye may know what is the hope
of his calling, and what the riches of the glory
of his inheritance in the saints, and what *is* the
exceeding greatness of his power toward us
who believe, according to the working of his
mighty power, which he wrought in Christ,
when he raised him from the dead, and set
him at his own right hand in the heavenly
places, far above all principality, and power,
and might, and dominion, and every name
that is named, not only in this world, but also
in that which is to come: and hath put all
things under his feet, and gave him *to be* the

head over all *things* to the church, which is his body, the fulness of him that filleth all in all.

2 SAMUEL 23:3

The God of Israel said, the Rock of Israel spake to me, He that ruleth over men *must be* just, ruling in the fear of God.

GENESIS 14:1–2, 10-16, 18-20

And it came to pass in the days of Amraphel king of Shinar, Arioch king of Ellasar, Chedorla-omer king of Elam, and Tidal king of nations; *that these* made war with Bera king of Sodom, and with Birsha king of Gomorrah, Shinab king of Admah, and Shemeber king of Zeboiim, and the king of Bela, which is Zoar. And the vale of Siddim *was full of* slime pits; and the kings of Sodom and Gomorrah fled, and fell there; and they that remained fled to the mountain. And they took all the goods of Sodom and Gomorrah, and all their victuals, and went their way. And they took Lot, Abram's brother's son, who dwelt in Sodom, and his goods, and departed. And there came one that had escaped, and told Abram the Hebrew; for he dwelt in the plain of Mamre the Amorite, brother of Eshcol, and brother of Aner: and these *were* confederate with Abram. And when Abram heard that his brother was taken captive, he armed his trained *servants*, born in his own house, three hundred and eighteen, and pursued *them* into Dan. And he divided himself against them, he and his servants, by night, and smote them, and pursued them unto Hobah, which *is* on the left hand of Damascus. And he brought back all the goods, and also brought again his brother Lot, and his goods, and the women also, and the people. And Melchizedek king of Salem brought forth bread and wine: and he *was* the priest of the most high God. And he blessed him, and said, Blessed *be* Abram of the most high God, possessor of heaven and earth: and blessed be the most high God, which hath delivered thine enemies into thy hand and He gave him tithes of all.

GENESIS 22:17

That in blessing I will bless thee, and in multiplying I will multiply thy seed as the stars of the heaven, and as the sand which *is* upon the sea shore; and thy seed shall possess the gate of his enemies;

LUKE 1:68-75

Blessed *be* the Lord God of Israel; for he hath visited and redeemed his people, and hath raised up an horn of salvation for us in the house of his servant David; as he spake by the mouth of his holy prophets, which have been since the world began: that we should be saved from our enemies, and from the hand of all that hate us; to perform the mercy *promised* to our fathers, and to remember his holy covenant; the oath which he swore to our father Abraham, that he would grant unto us, that we being delivered out of the hand of our enemies might serve him without fear, in holiness and righteousness before him, all the days of our life.

HEBREWS 7:1–2

For this Melchizedek, king of Salem, priest of the most high God, who met Abraham returning from the slaughter of the kings, and blessed him; to whom also Abraham gave a tenth part of all; first being by interpretation King of righteousness, and after that also King of Salem, which is, King of peace.

PSALM 149:6-9

Let the high *praises* of God *be* in their mouth, and a two-edged sword in their hand; to execute vengeance upon the heathen, *and* punishments upon the people; to bind their kings with chains, and their nobles with fetters of iron; to execute upon them the judgment written: this honor have all his saints. Praise ye the LORD.

PART TWO

The Purpose of the Sword

3

THE SWORD TO PUNISH EVIL

QUESTION:

Who originated civic or civil government among men?

ANSWER:

God. The powers that be, i.e., the offices of civil magistrates, are ordained of God. Civil government did not originate with man; it is not man's idea. Civil government originated with God, by God's directive.

QUESTION:

Is civil government the sole form of government God has established?

ANSWER:

No. God first established church government, then family government, then self-government, and finally civil government (see Gen. 2:7; 4:15). It is arguable that as the last, it is the least important.

QUESTION:

For what purpose has God instituted civic government among men?

ANSWER:

To bring terror and punishment to those that do evil.

QUESTION:

Why does God order that civil magistrates bring punishment and terror to evildoers?

ANSWER:

First, by this means wickedness and a general moral anarchy cannot prevail. Swift and just punishment of the wicked brings fear to the heart of other would-be evildoers. They shrink back from doing wicked deeds for fear that the punishment they have seen visited on others will befall them. As the Scripture says, after just punishment, "And all Israel shall hear, and fear, and shall do no more any such wickedness as this is among you" (Deut. 13:11). Or according to Romans 13:4b, "But if thou do that which is evil, be afraid; for he beareth not the sword in vain. . ." By this means, wickedness is suppressed. Consider this base example: if no law against theft existed, and no punishment followed, many more people would yield to the temptation to help themselves to other men's goods. Second, in a climate where evil behavior is swiftly punished and where the enemies of God do not rule, individual and societal righteousness and justice can flourish in peace (see Luke 1:68–75).

QUESTION:

What does God's Word call a civil ruler?

ANSWER:

A minister of God.

QUESTION

How does this civil minister of God differ from a minister of God in the church?

ANSWER:

The civil minister of God is to uphold the civic portion of the law of God. The civil minister is confined in his *office* to suppressing and punishing evil actions.

His office is not ordained to infringe in church government or affairs; i.e., he is not called to serve communion or bring church discipline. He is called to punish the evildoer for criminal deeds done or criminal words spoken. He is not ordained to punish individuals for private evil beliefs or for the neglect of righteous duty.

The minister of Christ's church—such as a pastor, elder, and/or teacher, apostle, prophet, etc. (see Eph. 4:11–12), has other responsibilities. For example, he is to preach the Word (which searches men's hearts), visit the sick, feed the poor, clothe the naked, minister to families, care for the orphan and the widow, herald Christ's gospel, rebuke the careless, and warn the unbeliever of eternal damnation (see I Tim. 4:2, Matt. 25:31–40, James 1:27, 1 Pet. 5:2, Heb. 13:7,17, Acts 20:17, 28–30, 1 Tim. 3:2–7, Titus 2:5–11).

The civil magistrate, *in his capacity as an individual Christian*, may show forth these acts of love and righteousness; he may beautify his office and the gospel by being a civil magistrate who loves God, who gives alms and serves holy communion. But by the power of his office—with the power of the sword—*he cannot lawfully compel citizens to show compassion to the poor and needy.* He may not take money by force of law or threat of force and give it to those he deems most needy; neither may he use his sword to preach the gospel and convert the lost to faith in Christ. Though the neglect of compassion and preaching is evil before God, it is not within the magistrate's Biblical authority to punish that neglect, nor to compel obedience by force.

QUESTION:

What deeds, then, can the civil magistrate punish?

ANSWER:

The civil magistrate is authorized to punish evil for which God has identified temporal punishment in His Word. These punishments are primarily capital, corporal, and restitution. He cannot go beyond this. The civil magistrate may punish murder (see, for example, Deut. 19:11–13, Exod. 21:22–25), but not hate. He may punish theft (see Exod. 22:9), but not covetousness. He may punish assaults (see Deut. 17:8–9), but not hardness of heart toward the poor.

If the Scripture forbids something or commands another thing, yet there is not corresponding civil punishment attached for disobedience, the civil ruler may not punish for it. "Oh! But how then will this evil be checked?" someone will ask. The evil deeds that are outside his jurisdiction will be dealt with by God—by His convincing Spirit, His Church, friends, family, neighbors, or even Providential chastening. God has many means of rebuking evil at His disposal. It is not for the civil ruler to play God.

QUESTION:

Why can't the civil magistrate punish all wrongs?

ANSWER:

God has not authorized him to do so. He must rule in the fear of God (see Exod. 18:21, Deut. 17:15–20). He must rule by the wisdom and law of God. That means He must rule according to the command-ments of the Lord. God outlines in His Word which sins are crimes to be punished by the civic magistrate. We are not to add to His Word lest He rebuke us and prove us liars (see Prov. 30:6).

Consider this illustration. God has commanded the preaching of the gospel, the baptism of Christians, the disciplining of children. Should the civic magis-trate—the government—choose our sermons, bap-tize us and our children, and apply the rod to our children? Of course not. This would create a culture in which "the state" was master of everyone's destiny; the state would be everyone's god, everyone's dad, everyone's savior. This, of course, is precisely what communist and socialist governments want—and what we are headed toward in America—the govern-ment as healer (national health care—Medicare, Medicaid), deliverer (new homes after flooding), provider (government housing and food stamps), etc. And one only need look at the oppression, mur-der, and suffering that has accompanied socialism worldwide to see the folly of our present course. Moreover, because the sword has been committed to the state (though not exclusively), the temptation to abuse this authority and to go beyond God's boundaries is ever present with civil governments. For the heart of man—even the best-meaning civil magistrate—is desperately wicked.

Question:

God has ordained through the civil magistrate's sword that evil deeds are suppressed and punished. What does the "sword" mean?

Answer:

"The sword" means (in part) the death sentence. That is, a sword is not used for spanking or other forms of discipline or punishment, but for death.

Question:

Are we to assume that all civic evil is to be punished by death?

Answer:

No. This is the *ultimate* earthly penalty, but not the *only* earthly penalty. In other instances the sword provides the power to enforce lesser penalties.

QUESTION:

What other punishments besides the death sentence may the civic minister of God bring?

ANSWER:

Those prescribed by God's Law. For example, the thief should pay restitution *to the victim* (two-fold, four-fold, or five-fold, depending on the crime). The assailant should receive a corporal punishment commensurate with his crime—eye for eye, tooth for tooth, blow for blow. In some cases, *at the discretion of the victim*, the criminal may pay restitution to the victim, such as a sum of money for the victim's lost eye (since he will be inhibited in his work). The Bible also gives the parameters for corporal punishment, e.g., forty lashes less one (see 2 Cor. 11:24, Deut. 25:3, Ex. 21:28–30).

Furthermore, the Law authorizes men to be fined (or even executed) for civil liability or what we would call gross or criminal negligence. In these instances, the power of the sword is the power to ensure that the punishment is carried out, that the criminal submits to the penalty.

QUESTION:

Why can the civil magistrate not prescribe the punishment he feels is best? For example, why can he not cut off a thief's hand?

ANSWER:

God's Law cannot be annulled or improved on by mortal, sinful man. It is sheer arrogance to believe that we could come up with "justice" (so-called) that would be more just than God's justice and judgments. A civil magistrate may never in the name of "justice" execute a thief nor cut off his hand. Neither can a murderer buy back his life. Such "punishments" would be *evil*, for they go against the clear Word of God.

QUESTION:

Are jails in the Bible, and if so, are they ordained for punishment?

ANSWER:

There is a record of jails in the Bible as punishment, in pagan Egypt (see Gen. 41), backslidden Israel (see the books of Jeremiah and the story of Micah), and in New Testament times (see the Book of Acts). It appears the Jews also used jails to hold prisoners until trial (a trial which was to be *very speedy*). However, *nowhere in the Law of God are jails or prisons listed as a punishment ordained of God*. Incarceration for punishment is a man-made menace, a twisted form of slavery which does not reflect God's justice.

However, one form of "detention" in the Law was prescribed. If a man stole something and could not pay the restitution demanded, and his family did not pay it for him, he was sold for his theft. He then worked as an indentured servant until the debt was paid.

For those who feel this is cruel or unjust, consider this: tens of thousands, perhaps hundreds of thousands, of citizens are rotting in jails and prisons across our nation for theft. Furthermore, multiple thousands of them are working for slave wages (11 cents per hour, for example) for state and federally owned manufacturing plants—manufacturing furniture, electronic hardware, clothing, etc. These prisons are *de facto* slave labor camps. And the government keeps the profits! The victims get *nothing!*

Meanwhile, a very high percentage of those incarcerated who are married wind up divorced; a large percentage of their families end up on welfare—costing the taxpayer more money; and tens of thousands of children become fatherless, with all its well-documented attending miseries. The family is punished for the father's sin.

Compare this to Biblical indentured servitude for theft restitution. First, the thief is able to take his family with him. Thus, he and they are not deprived of the tenderness of family life. The thief is not hurled into a culture of murderers, assaulters, drug pushers, and sex-offenders. Nor are the children and wife punished with such severity for the father's crime.

Children still have a daddy on hand, and a wife still has her husband.

Second, the taxpayers are not unjustly burdened with the financial obligations of paying for his incarceration and paying for welfare. In fact, it could be argued that extracting such monies from taxpayers for such purposes is a form of theft! As earlier stated, we cannot be compelled by the sword to show compassion (for example, state welfare), nor should we be compelled to pay for an unjust punishment on a thief, which also punishes innocent family members. And consider this—if a man has his watch or car stolen—what does he want? A new watch or car! How does the victim of theft benefit from a thief sitting in jail?

Finally, the proceeds from sales of goods the man produces during his enslavement repays his master for money that went to the *victim, not the state.* The victim is the one who had the loss; the victim should receive restitution. The debt is owed to the *victim—* not the state.

QUESTION:

What about a "debt to society"? Should a criminal pay fines to the civil magistrate?

ANSWER:

Nowhere in the Bible is punishment for criminal behavior called a "debt to society." The debt is owed to the *victim.* That is why (when applicable) the criminal pays the victim restitution or "fines." We might ask ourselves: *if criminals are paying a "debt to society," then why is society paying the debt?*

QUESTION:

How does a civil magistrate please God?

ANSWER:

"He hath showed thee, O man, what is good; and what doth the LORD require of thee, but to do justly, and to love mercy, and to walk humbly with thy God?" (Mic. 6:8).

The civil magistrate must faithfully execute his duties as God has outlined them in His Word. He must never take a bribe (see Exod. 23:8, Isa. 1:23). He must not show respect of persons. He must not favor the rich because he is rich, nor the poor because he is poor (Ezek. 45:9). He must rule or judge in the fear of God, knowing he will give account to God for his actions. He must cleave to that which is good and hate that which is evil.

QUESTION:

Where does one learn what is good or evil?

ANSWER:

The Holy Bible. Only God's Holy Word is authorized to define good and evil, righteousness and wickedness.

QUESTION:

*Is the civil magistrate free in a modern society,
a non-Jewish society, to determine for himself
that which is evil?*

ANSWER:

He is not free to determine right and wrong for himself, else the whole of Scripture would be abandoned. God alone can determine good and evil, and He has outlined this in His Law. The confused Christian or unbeliever who believes Mosaic Law was just for ancient Israel should remember these words of Christ and Paul the Apostle:

> Whosoever therefore shall break one of these least commandments, and shall teach men so, he shall be called the least in the kingdom of heaven: but whosoever shall do and teach them, the same shall be called great in the kingdom of heaven. (Matt. 5:19)

> Woe unto you, scribes and Pharisees, hypocrites! for ye pay tithe of mint and anise and cummin, and have omitted the weightier matters of the law, judgment, mercy, and faith: these ought ye to have done, and not to leave the other undone. (Matt. 23:23)

> But we know that the law is good, if a man use it lawfully; knowing this, that the law is not made for a righteous man, but for the lawless and disobedient, for the ungodly and for sin-

ners, for unholy and profane, for murderers of fathers and murderers of mothers, for manslayers. (1 Tim. 1:8–9)

What shall we say then? Is the law sin? God forbid. Nay, I had not known sin, but by the law: for I had not known lust, except the law had said, thou shalt not covet. (Rom. 7:7)

Wherefore the law was our schoolmaster to bring us unto Christ, that we might be justified by faith. (Gal. 3:24)

All Scripture is given by inspiration of God, and is profitable for doctrine, for reproof, for correction, for instruction in righteousness: that the man of God may be perfect, thoroughly furnished unto all good works. (2 Tim. 3:16–17)

Do we then nullify the Law through faith? May it never be! On the contrary, we establish the Law. (Rom. 3:31)

QUESTION:

Can the magistrate proclaim an act as evil and criminal that God has ordained as good, such as a parent's spanking his or her children?

ANSWER:

No. He cannot make crooked that which God has made straight. "Woe unto them that call evil good, and good evil; that put darkness for light, and light for darkness; that put bitter for sweet, and sweet for bitter!" (Isa. 5:20). Furthermore, if the Law of God is discarded as the standard, a civil ruler—*and each successive civil ruler*-would be free to be a god and lawmaker unto himself. Human law would become completely arbitrary.

4

THE SWORD TO OVERTHROW TYRANTS

QUESTION:

Does the civil minister of God in Romans 13 have unlimited authority?

ANSWER:

No. He is a minister of God; i.e., he is below God's jurisdiction and under God's authority. Only God is Sovereign, and God has said that all thrones and authorities were created *for* Him:

> . . . for by him were all things created, that are in heaven, and that are in earth, visible and

invisible, whether *they be* thrones, or domin-
ions, or principalities, or powers: all things
were created by him, and for him. (Col. 1:16)

. . . which he wrought in Christ, when he
raised him from the dead, and set *him* at his
own right hand in the heavenly *places*, far
above all principality, and power, and might,
and dominion, and every name that is named,
not only in this world, but also in that which
is to come: and hath put all *things* under his
feet, and gave him *to be* the head over all *things*
to the church, which is his body, the fulness
of him that filleth all in all. (Eph. 1:20–23)

QUESTION:

*What further Biblical reasonings or examples
can be given to show that the minister of God
in Romans 13 does not have unlimited power
and authority?*

ANSWER:

In Hebrews, the church of God is commanded to
"Obey them that have the rule over you, and submit
yourselves: for they watch for your souls, as they that
must give account" (Heb. 13:17a). Paul exhorted the
elders of the church at Ephesus saying, "Take heed
therefore unto yourselves, and to all the flock, over the
which the Holy Ghost hath made you overseers . . . "
(Acts 20:28). These passages show that elders in

churches have a certain level of authority over peoples' lives.

However, the pastors and elders in our midst cannot use this authority for a cloak of wickedness (see 1 Pet. 5:1–5). For example, if a pastor of a congregation to whom oversight and authority is given should command a thing that is contrary to God's Word, he is not to be obeyed. If the pastor preaches heresy, he is to be censored, and if he cleaves to his heresy, he is stripped of his authority and excommunicated. If a pastor were to commit theft, he should be punished according to law; he is not permitted to steal because he is God's minister.

In short, we see that the pastor—a "minister of God," holding an office of honor and authority ordained by God—does not have unlimited power and authority, but he is subject to the demands and constraints of God's Law and the whole of the Scriptures.

Likewise, a civic magistrate should not place himself, nor be placed by others, above the Law of God. Why would Christians grant a civic minister of God a level of autonomy from God and His Law that we would never give to an ecclesiastical minister of God? Why would we grant kings or princes a level of "free reign" that would put their word and law above the very Word and Law of God? God gives them no such liberties but instead solemnly warns them:

> Be wise now therefore, O ye kings: be instructed, ye judges of the earth. Serve the LORD with fear, and rejoice with trembling. Kiss the Son, lest he be angry, and ye perish *from* the way, when his wrath is kindled but a

little. Blessed *are* all they that put their trust in him. (Ps. 2:10–12)

QUESTION:

What if the civic magistrate permits or promotes evil?

ANSWER:

If he permits evil, he is derelict in his duty and sins against God. If he promotes evil, he is in greater rebellion against God and has betrayed the purpose of his office.

QUESTION:

If the magistrate orders citizens to follow him in his sin, are the citizens bound to obey?

ANSWER:

In the area of his rebellion, they need not obey. As Peter said, to rebellious rulers of his day, "...Whether it be right in the sight of God to hearken unto you more than unto God, judge ye" and "...We ought to obey God rather than men" (Acts 4:19, 5:29). A civic magistrate can never claim it is the citizen's duty to follow him more than God. (See also the Hebrew midwives in Exod. 1:15–21; Rahab the harlot in Josh. 2:1–21, 6:23–25; the wise men in Matt. 2:7–12; the three Hebrew children in Dan. 3:8–30.)

QUESTION:

What of those who say we must obey all magistrates for conscience sake, as the text says (Rom. 13:6)?

ANSWER:

They misread the text, for it plainly says that the civil magistrate's duty is to punish the wicked for evil deeds. The civil magistrate has no authority from God to order the citizens to commit acts of wickedness, neither is he authorized to punish the righteous for righteous deeds. That would be treachery and villainy against God, His church, and His clearly revealed Word. And certainly God does not want us to follow a civil magistrate down a path of sin and death.

Let us use this illustration to further emphasize the point. If a pagan prince makes a law for citizens to worship him or burn incense to him or bow before an image of himself, does he have the authority from God to make such a law? Does God annul or suspend the first and second commandments in order to please this wicked tyrant? Would God say that His people should revere and bow before this false deity? God forbid! The three Hebrew children, Daniel the prophet, and the early church martyrs present us with abundant testimony that we cannot—in the name of "conscience"—do that which offends our conscience, and more importantly, offends our Great and Sovereign God.

QUESTION:

What if the civil magistrate continually neglects the duty of his office? What if he chastises the righteous but lets the deeds of the wicked flourish under his protection?

ANSWER:

If such a civil magistrate should use his office and sword for theft, rapine, murder, or the general oppression of the people, he stands condemned of the Law as a thief, a murderer, and an evildoer; and he should thus be treated. He himself is under the Law. But he is much more than a common malefactor, because by reason of the virtue and honor and authority associated with his office, he multiplies his wickedness many times over. In fact, he becomes an example of corruption, a leader of rebellion against heaven's law, and a hero and champion of evildoers. From the stature of his office flows a unique power to inspire or strengthen other rebels in acts of evil, to put dread in the hearts of the righteous, and to help the wicked spring up and bloom.

And for this his sin against God and man is all the greater.

> Woe unto them that decree unrighteous decrees, and that write grievousness *which* they have prescribed; to turn aside the needy from judgment, and to take away the right from the poor of my people, that widows may be their

prey, and *that* they may rob the fatherless! (Isa. 10:1–2)

Shall the throne of iniquity have fellowship with thee, which frameth mischief by a law? (Ps. 94:20)

Biblical (and extra-biblical) history shows the insidiously destructive impact a wicked magistrate (or magistrates) can have on a nation. Under Manasseh, the most hideous crimes flourished, including child-sacrifice and ritual homosexual prostitution inside Solomon's temple; the true worship of God faltered and nearly perished (see 2 Kings 21—24:4). Under Ahab and Jezebel, the prophets of Baal and all their attending wickednesses thrived. Under Athaliah, the land was troubled, and the temple fell into ruin. The lesson is clear: when an evil king reigned, evil flourished in the land, and righteousness and peace suffered.

QUESTION:

What should the people of God do when an evil magistrate or magistrates (or government) is wreaking havoc in a nation?

ANSWER:

"If the foundations be destroyed, what can the righteous do?" (Ps. 11:3). The people of God should pray for the conversion of, or for the judgment of God to come on, such wicked leaders (see Ps. 94). The people of God should cry out for deliverance (see Exod.

2:23–25). They should resist the spread of evil (see Prov. 28:4) and refuse to obey unlawful orders (see Acts 4:19, 5:29). Furthermore, they should seek his removal by peaceful means and replace him with a righteous magistrate (see the examples of David and Saul, Solomon, Jereboam and Rehoboam).

QUESTION:

And what if the evil magistrate(s) cannot be peacefully dislodged from power, and they continue to wreak havoc on the people? If a lower magistrate or a group of magistrates raises a revolution against a wicked, unrepentant magistrate, is it ever lawful to join them in the pursuit of revolution by the sword?

ANSWER:

Yes, as a last resort. Psalm 149 gives clear testimony that God's people may—with a two-edged sword— "bind their kings with chains, and their nobles with fetters of iron; to execute upon them the judgment written: this honor have all his saints. . . " (Ps. 149:8–9).

In other examples we see God raised up the prophets Elijah and Elisha to confront Ahab and Jezebel, and then He raised up Jehu to overthrow and destroy their house with the sword (see 1 Kings 18–2 Kings 10). The wicked murderous Queen Athaliah reigned in Judah for six years. In the seventh year, Jehoiada the high priest with certain captains raised an insurrection against her and had her executed (see 2 Kings 11:4–16).

In the American Revolution, Knox's Revolution, and Cromwell's Revolution, lower magistrates, businessmen, "elders in the gate," and the people themselves fought against and overthrew wicked princes in accordance with God's Word. In this was God honored.

QUESTION:

But what of those who say we should never take up the sword? Did not Jesus say ". . . They that take the sword shall perish with the sword" (Matt. 26:52)?

ANSWER:

To the whole of Scripture they must go.

Consider the first "war" in the Bible, which was followed by the clearest "type" of Christ in the Bible and perhaps the first theophany. (First occurrences or "first things" are very important in building theology.) This is recorded in Genesis 19.

The kings of Sodom and Gomorrah (and three other kings) were attacked and overrun by Chedorlaomer and three other kings. Their inhabitants, including Lot and his family, were taken captive. Abraham learned of the defeat and pursued Chedorlaomer with three hundred and eighteen armed servants, men trained in the use of arms in Abraham's house. He was accompanied by Mamre and Aner. (This, by the way, is the Biblical starting point for the doctrine of just war, as well as the right of private citizens to own weapons.) Abraham and his men overtook these armies, slaughtered the kings, and rescued Lot—*all with the sword.* When "returning from the slaughter of the kings" (see Heb. 7:1), Abraham was met by Melchizedek—King of righteousness, King of peace, Priest of the Most High God—believed by some theologians to be a Christophany (a pre-incarnation appearance of Christ Himself).

Melchizedek blessed Abraham saying, "... Blessed be Abram of the most high God, possessor of heaven and earth: and blessed be the most high God, which hath delivered thine enemies into thy hand..." (Gen. 14:19–20). It is clear that Almighty God delivered the wicked kings into Abram's hand to be slaughtered by his sword. Could not the quote of Christ "... for all they that take the sword shall perish with the sword" (Matt. 26:52) be applied here? Those who live by the sword (like the evil kings) shall die by the sword (at the hands of righteous Abram).

After being blessed, Abram gave Melchizedek a tithe of all the spoils, which Melchizedek received. This signified that the booty (and the subsequent tithe) were obtained in a manner acceptable and pleasing to God.

This slaughter of the kings was prompted by their unjust seizure of persons and property (such as Lot and his family—a type of the church). Abraham did not recognize Chedorlaomer's authority to do this, and he pursued and slaughtered him and his allies with the help of God and the subsequent blessing of Melchizedek.

That Melchizedek should show himself at the slaughter of the kings is critically important. Psalm 110 says of Christ: "The LORD hath sworn, and will not repent, Thou *art* a priest for ever after the order of Melchizedek" (v. 4). The very next verse says, "The Lord at thy right hand shall strike through kings in the day of his wrath" (v. 5). The Psalm also states that "Thy people shall be willing in the day of thy power." (v. 3)—willing to stand with Christ the King in His reign, willing to stand against wicked princes.

And so we have this lesson from Genesis 14, Hebrews 7, Psalm 110, Psalm 2, Psalm 149, and from many examples in the Scriptures: if a wicked prince by habitual and stiff-necked rebellion fails in the God-ordained duty of his office to uphold God's Law, if he proves instead a terror to the righteous and a comfort and benefactor to evildoers, if the gospel is suppressed, if the citizens are harassed and have their lives, liberty, and property perpetually in danger— and if such a prince (or government) is given a season for repentance, and he refuses to repent— then it is the right and perhaps even the duty of other magistrates and the people (in good order and discipline under God's Law) to overthrow such a tyrant.

One further note concerning Christ's rebuke of Peter when Peter cut off the ear of the high priest's servant. It is clear from Scripture that Christ had to die; it was the predestined will of God. So whether by flight, by bribery, by subtlety, by negotiation, or by sword, it was not God's will for the apostles to deliver Christ from death. For Jesus told Pilate, ". . . My kingdom is not *of* [i.e., not *from* here in origin] this world. If my kingdom were of this world, my servants would fight, so that I should not be delivered to the Jews; but now my kingdom is not from here"(John 18:36). Christ needed to die at that juncture to effect salvation. To deliver Christ from death would have been to fight against the will of God.

Finally, this theology concerning the sword is that which undergirded Knox, Cromwell, and the signers of the Declaration. This is why the Reformation survived. This is why (in part) we have a Bible in our mother tongue. This theology fueled the religious fervor, the prayers, the sermons, and writings of the "Black Regiment"—the nickname the American clergy were given by British soldiers because they withstood King George's authority during the American Revolution. For a Christian to reject this line of reasoning is to reject the underlying philosophy and theology of our freedom. (It is worth noting that 80 percent of the political tracts of the 1760s and 1770s were written by Christian ministers. Would to God we had that level of courage and adroitness today.)

Those Christians who reject this theology are in effect saying that they condemn the Declaration of Independence and the subsequent American Revolution as an unlawful rebellion, that they condemn George Washington for being a rebel, and in effect that the United States should still be united with the British crown. Is that what you believe?

QUESTION:

When, then, should the people of God and the citizenry seek the overthrow of a certain magistrate or civil government?

ANSWER:

This, of course, is the most practical and at times the most pressing question to be asked.

John Knox and the Scottish reformers gave Mary Stuart (Mary, Queen of Scots) much grace and patience while they knew she was plotting against them. Several small uprisings checked her wicked intentions, yet she remained on the throne. Only when she was implicated in adultery and the murder of her husband did they overthrow her and clamor for her head—which was eventually severed from her body while in exile in England by order of her cousin, Queen Elizabeth. Two generations later, Parliament and Cromwell defeated King Charles I in the civil war, yet they then attempted to work out a compromise with him. His constant treachery and his seeking of foreign kings to invade England to crush parliamentary forces led to his trial and execution.

The Declaration of Independence stated that the colonists—and all men—"are more disposed to suffer, while evils are sufferable, than to right themselves by abolishing the forms to which they are accustomed."

Let us look at Biblical history for examples of the "timing" of rebellion:

Eglon, King of Moab, ruled and oppressed Israel for eighteen years before God raised up Ehud to kill him and lead the overthrow of Moabite rule over Israel (see Judg. 3).

The Midianites, led by Sisera, oppressed Israel for seven years before God raised up Gideon to overthrow them (see Judg. 4–8).

Athaliah reigned over Judah for seven years before the priest Jehoiada raised an insurrection against her and had her executed (see 2 Kings 11).

David fled from Saul for years—*and was not permitted by God to kill him.* God took Saul's life in a battle against the Philistines (see 1 Sam. 18–31).

The four kings who attacked and captured Sodom, Lot, et al were immediately fought and slaughtered (see Gen. 14:17).

So we see from these passages (and others) and from the historical examples that the timing of the overthrow and demise of tyrants may vary widely.

QUESTION:

Does the Scripture show any principles or tokens of Providence when such a time might be?

Yes. These providential tokens are related to the heart of the people. Are the people righteous? Are they wicked? Did their own sin give rise to a tyrant? Are they repentant?

QUESTION:

Are you saying that tyrants may have arisen as a judgment of God on a wicked people?

ANSWER:

Yes. The Books of the Law (Genesis, Exodus, Leviticus, Numbers and Deuteronomy—also known as the Pentateuch) give the Covenantal reasons and principles for the *rise* as well as the *overthrow* of tyrants.

The historical and prophetic books give the application of these principles and different scenarios surrounding the rise, reign, and inevitable demise of tyrants.

The Book of Judges gives many concise illustrations of the topic in discussion. Let us consider some of these principles and illustrations.

First, the reign of a wicked, oppressive regime over a people is often the judgment of God on the wickedness of a nation. For example:

> And the children of Israel did evil in the sight of the LORD, and served Baalim: and they forsook the LORD God of their fathers, which brought them out of the land of Egypt, and followed other gods, of the gods of the people that were round about them, and bowed themselves unto them, and provoked the LORD to anger. And they forsook the LORD, and served Baal and Ashtaroth. And the anger of the LORD was hot against Israel, and he

delivered them into the hands of spoilers that spoiled them, and he sold them into the hands of their enemies round about, so that they could not any longer stand before their enemies. (Judg. 2:11–14)

And the children of Israel did evil again in the sight of the LORD: and the LORD strengthened Eglon the king of Moab against Israel, because they had done evil in the sight of the LORD. (Judg. 3:12)

And the children of Israel again did evil in the sight of the LORD, when Ehud was dead. And the LORD sold them into the hand of Jabin king of Canaan, that reigned in Hazor; the captain of whose host *was* Sisera, which dwelt in Harosheth of the Gentiles. And the children of Israel cried unto the LORD: for he had nine hundred chariots of iron; and twenty years he mightily oppressed the children of Israel. (Judg. 4:1–3)

God Himself may raise up a wicked tyrant to chasten the people for their sin; He causes the citizenry to groan under the burden of oppressive government, to prompt—or extract—repentance from them. Hardship and trial often result in deep self-analysis, leading to repentance.

Second, when a significant portion or remnant of the people repent of the sins that gave rise to the tyranny and cry out to God for mercy (and it is God who determines what is a significant remnant), He forgives them and invigorates them to overthrow the wicked king or nation that is oppressing them.

> So the children of Israel served Eglon the king of Moab eighteen years. But when the children of Israel cried unto the LORD, the LORD raised them up a deliverer, Ehud the son of Gera, a Benjamite, a man left-handed. . . . And Ehud put forth his left hand, and took the dagger from his right thigh, and thrust it into his (Eglon's) belly.. . . he blew a trumpet in the mountain of Ephraim, and the children of Israel went down with him from the mount, and he before them. And he said unto them, Follow after me: for the LORD hath delivered your enemies the Moabites into your hand. And they went down after him, and took the fords of Jordan toward Moab, and suffered not a man to pass over. So Moab was subdued that day under the hand of Israel... (Judg. 3:14, 15a, 21, 27–28, 30)

> And the LORD sold them into the hand of Jabin king of Canaan, that reigned in Jazor; the captain of whose host *was* Sisera, which dwelt in Harosheth of the Gentiles. And the children of Israel cried unto the LORD: for he had nine hundred chariots of iron; and twenty years he mightily oppressed the children of Israel.... And Deborah said to Barak, "Arise! For this is the day in which the LORD has given Sisera into your hands; behold, the Lord has gone out before you." So Barak went

down from Mount Tabor with ten thousand men following him. And the LORD routed Sisera and all his chariots and all his army, with the edge of the sword before Barak; and Sisera alighted from his chariot and fled away on foot. (Judges 4:2-3; 14:14–15)

And Israel was greatly impoverished because of the Midianites; and the children of Israel cried unto the LORD. . . . And the Lord looked at him and said, "Go in this your strength and deliver [Gideon] Israel from the hand of Midian. Have I not sent you?" So Midian was subdued before the sons of Israel, and they did not lift up their heads anymore. And the land was undisturbed for forty years in the days of Gideon. (Judg. 6:6; 6:14–16; 8:28)

It is interesting to note that God raised up the oppressors to chasten His people but then chose to remove the oppressors by the sword of His people.

Third, sometimes rebellions against an evil king or nation are ill-timed and sometimes rebellions are led by evil men. If so, they will fail, or the revolution will be oppressive and perhaps more tyrannical than its predecessor. For example, Ishmael, who was the son of Nethaniah, killed Gedaliah, who was the Jewish governor of Judah appointed by Nebuchadnezzar. But this murder and revolt did *nothing* to break the Babylonian yoke from their necks (see Jer. 41). After the death of Gideon, Israel again practiced wickedness:

And it came to pass, as soon as Gideon was dead, that the children of Israel turned again, and went a whoring after Baalim, and made Baal-berith their god. And the children of Israel remembered not the LORD their God, who had delivered them out of the hands of all their enemies on every side: neither showed they kindness to the house of Jerub-baal, *namely*, Gideon, according to all the goodness which he had showed unto Israel. (Judg. 8:33–35)

In that hour, Abimelech, son of Gideon by a concubine, rose up with the men of Shechem and wickedly slew all his brothers, the sons of Gideon, in order to make himself a king. Three years later, God judged him and the men of Shechem for their cruelty; they were slain in bitter battles (see Judg. 9). Their rebellion produced no righteous fruit.

This is a critically important point when analyzing (historically or contemporarily) a tyrannical prince or government and a revolution. A government may be corrupt-but the people may be more corrupt. If a rebellion occurs at such a time, the ensuing events simply cannot bear widespread righteous fruit. One area of oppression may be exchanged for another.

The French Revolution gives perfect clarity to this principle. Louis XVI was overthrown by a horribly immoral people. The result was vandalism, theft, rapine, bloodshed, and murder—random chaos and cruelty that far exceeded any injustice committed by Louis XVI did. (The French Revolution was a godless, lawless revolution, not the root of modern freedoms as some lying humanists would tell us—unless they mean "freedom" from God's Law). The French Revolution was the father of Communism. (See *Robespierre: The Fool as a Revolutionary*, The Reformer Library, 1995.)

Likewise, consider the Revolution of the Bolsheviks against Nicholas the Czar. The communists used lying rhetoric of justice, mercy, brotherhood, etc. (terms stolen from Christianity)—but their revolution was godless, lawless, bloody, and oppressive.

Fourth, the righteous use of the sword to overthrow tyrants was not chaotic in the sense of striking blindly, but it was against certain people to restore certain freedoms and specific boundaries. The Israelites did not try to conquer the world. They did not try to take land that God had not given them. Furthermore, to again look at the Cromwellian Revolution-his victories were not marred by theft, murder, and rapine. Frankly, this is perhaps the most amazing mark left by Cromwell's soldiers in the history of military conquest. Cromwell's "New Model Army" was a group largely comprised of praying men; they were devout Christians who were godly, disciplined, and merciful to non-combatants.

Finally, it is significant that God raises up a point man or point men to lead the overthrow of wicked government. For example, Samson delivered Israel; later Gideon delivered Israel. Deborah and Shamgar, son of Anath, were contemporary judges. In American history we see George Washington as the leader in the field of battle, while the signers declared war.

Likewise Cromwell was in the field with other generals, and the Parliament had raised the army against Charles I.

In the light of the Biblical examples of the use of the sword to overthrow tyrants God has given us in the historical and prophetic books; in the light of the authority of Christ—"All power (authority) is given unto me in heaven and in earth" (Matt. 28:18b); knowing that all thrones were created by Him and for Him—for His pleasure and glory (see Eph. 1:20 and Col. 1:18); knowing that He commands all kings everywhere to serve Him (see Ps. 2); knowing that kings who refuse to serve Him may see His wrath flare up and thus be destroyed in the way or struck through in His wrath (see Ps. 2 and 110); and knowing that Christ reigns in the order of Melchizedek (see Ps. 110; Heb. 7), we may safely conclude the following:

- A people—domestic and/or foreign—may tell a wicked, oppressive king or government to repent of tyranny and evil and to uphold the Law of God.

- The people of God may justly cry out to God for deliverance; i.e., the tyrant's conversion, removal, and/or destruction.

- A righteous people under righteous leadership should work for the removal and replacement of wicked leaders.

- As a last resort they may take up the sword to overthrow the tyrannical regime that oppresses them or oppresses their neighbor or brother.

- The timing and means of such revolution (as seen in the Scriptures) vary by Providence from situation to situation. No "cast in stone" formula for timing and means exists for lawful revolution. What does exist are the principles of Genesis 14; Psalms 2, 110, and 149; and Romans 13. The people of God must cry out to Him for His guidance and His gracious and merciful Providence.

5

CHRIST REIGNS *NOW*

I must again reiterate that I view this effort as a starting point for thoughtful Bible study. I fully recognize that this work is not in any way comprehensive. I also realize that I may have provoked more questions than I have answered. So be it.

I rest confident that I have pointed you to the right book to resolve the questions—the Bible. And I am confident before God that I have carried on the discussion of the sword and of submission to civil magistrates and the overthrow of tyrants at the biblical starting points that the Scripture gives us. Those texts are clear, their meaning is clear, and the discussion (I believe) must issue forth from this framework—that Christ is the reigning monarch of the earth. If you contend that this is the devil's world, we cannot even have a constructive discussion or debate. We believe in a different revelation about the power and majesty and sovereignty of God.

It is my hope that the truths herein discussed have strengthened and blessed you. I hope that you have seen the divine origin of civil government and that you more clearly see the authority of civil government to suppress and punish evil deeds—so that righteousness and the righteous may flourish. I hope that you consider striving for civil office yourself or that you dedicate yourself to helping other godly men and women attain to such offices.

I must pause and state clearly that the Bible (and this author's work) presupposes that God's people should be involved in, yeah, the leaders, in civic government. Those misguided souls in the church who draw unbiblical divisions between the sacred and secular, this world and the next—and in so many words tells us to let this world and its governments go to hell—are simply not speaking from the authority of the Scriptures. Worse yet, they are part of the problem. The "escapist" or "separatist" mentality that has dominated much of the church (in doctrine or practice) in America is a prime reason why America is in crisis. We are the salt that has lost is savor, and we are being trampled underfoot. It is a Christian duty to participate in cultural service and leadership. For further study on this topic, read *The Micah Mandate*, by George Grant (Moody Press 1995).

One other critical point must be made. On occasion, you may hear someone flippantly say, "What we need is another American Revolution." When I hear that, I respond, "If we have run against footmen and grown weary, how can we prevail against horses?" Our constitutional forum of representative government is a glorious safeguard against the last resort— the sword. Those who have not voted, those social sluggards in our pews who have never lifted a finger to replace an evil politician with a righteous statesman, have little ground to discuss the feasability of Revolution.

I also hope this enables you to study the history of righteous and evil revolutions through the grid of God's Law and Christ's reign. Furthermore, I earnestly hope that with these truths you will be able to refute and silence those deadly foes of liberty in our midst, those in the church who would have us submit to every tyrant forever—rendering us as prey and ultimately the slaves of the "state." The well-meaning but deceived Christian leaders who call for nearly unconditional obedience to tyrants—those who insist Christians have no right or duty to ever overthrow tyrants—are unwitting collaborators with the enemies of God. They are also the delight of tyrants, for they are useful in calming the angry citizenry. They validate all oppression of tyrants as coming from the hand of God.

Another critical point should be made here. The recent bombings in Oklahoma City were terrorism; vile, treacherous, murderous acts. The guilty should be publicly executed. Such attacks have no theological or philosophical connection to our discussion. On the contrary—such acts are cut from the cloth of the French Revolution—where terrorism and the slaughter of the innocent were standard fare. The rules of

"Christian warefare" layed out for centuries in Christendom clearly taught that you do not deliberately kill non-combatants and you show mercy to your captured enemies. (I state this only because some Joseph Goebbels-type propoganda expert in the press will probably say the viewpoints expressed in this book are responsible for these bombings.

And finally, should the hour come in any nation in the earth that Providence calls on Christians and lovers of liberty to break off the yoke of tyrants, may these Biblical truths help them obtain the resolution and the strength of conscience equal to the hour.

In the Name of God, the only Sovereign, King of kings, and Lord of Lords may the banners be raised. Amen.

Now let us examine certain documents, speeches, words, that embody the principles of the sword we have discussed. As you will see, this was not classroom debate; but rather courageous men taking enormous risks, shedding real blood, to obtain cherished freedom. And whether you know it or not, if you are a Christian, this is your heritage.

So take courage and learn from their examples.

PART THREE

The History of the Sword

6

GIVE ME LIBERTY

PATRICK HENRY'S "GIVE ME LIBERTY" SPEECH, AMERICA 1775

Source: William Wirt Henry, *Patrick Henry Life, Correspondence and Speeches*, Volume 1 (Harrisonburg, Virginia: Sprinkle Publications, 1993), 261-66.

Condensed version of Patrick Henry's speech in regards to arming the colony gathered from the recollections of Judges John Tyler and St. George Tucker:

"He rose at this time with a majesty unusual to him in an exordium, and with all that self-possession by which he was so invariably distinguished. 'No man,' he said, 'thought more highly than he did of the patriotism, as well as abilities, of the very worthy gentlemen who had just addressed the house. But different men often saw the same subject in different lights; and therefore, he hoped it would not be thought disrespectful to those gentlemen, if, entertaining, as he did, opinions of a character very opposite to theirs, he should speak forth *his* sentiments freely, and without reserve. 'This,' he said, 'was no time for ceremony. The question before the house was one of awful moment to this country. For his own part, he considered it as nothing less than a question of freedom or slavery. And in proportion to the magnitude of the subject, ought to be the freedom of debate. It was only in this way that they could hope to arrive at truth, and fulfil the great responsibility which they held to God and their country. Should he keep back his opinions at such a time, through fear of giving offense, he should consider himself guilty of treason toward his country, and of an act of disloyalty toward the majesty of Heaven, which he revered above all earthly kings.

"'Mr. President,' said he, 'it is natural to man to indulge in the illusions of hope. We are apt to shut our eyes against a painful truth-and listen to the song of that syren, till she transforms us into beasts. Is this,' he asked, 'the part of wise men, engaged in a great and arduous struggle for liberty? Were we disposed to be of the number of those, who having eyes, see not, and having ears, hear not, the things which so nearly concern their temporal salvation? For his part, whatever anguish of spirit it might cost, *he* was willing to know the whole truth; to know the worst, and to provide for it.'

'"He had,' he said, 'but one lamp by which his feet were guided; and that was the lamp of experience. He knew of no way of judging the future but by the past. And judging by the past, he wished to know what there had been in the conduct of the British ministry for the last ten years, to justify those hopes with which gentlemen had been pleased to solace themselves and the house? Is it that insidious smile with which our petition has been lately received? Trust it not, sir; it will prove a snare to your feet. Suffer not yourselves to be betrayed with a kiss. Ask yourselves how this gracious reception of our petition comports with those warlike preparations which cover our waters and darken our land. Are fleets and armies necessary to a work of love and reconciliation? Have we shown ourselves so unwilling to be reconciled, that force must be called in to win back our love? Let us not deceive ourselves, sir. These are the implements of war and subjugation-the last arguments to which kings resort. I ask gentlemen, sir, what means this martial array, if its purpose be not to force us to submission? Can gentlemen assign any other possible motive for it? Has Great Britain any enemy in this quarter of the world, to call for all this accumulation of navies and armies? No, sir, she has none. They are meant for us: they can be meant for no other. They are sent over to bind and rivet upon us those chains, which the British ministry have been so long forging. And what have we to oppose to them? Shall we try argument? Sir, we have been trying that for the last ten years. Have we anything new to offer upon the subject? Nothing. We have held the subject up in every light of which it is capable; but it has been all in vain. Shall we resort to entreaty and humble supplication? What terms shall we find, which have not been already exhausted? Let us not, I beseech you, sir, deceive ourselves longer. Sir, we have done everything that could be done, to avert the storm which is now coming on. We have petitioned—we have remonstrated—we have supplicated—we have prostrated ourselves before the throne, and have implored its interposition to arrest the tyrannical hands of the ministry and parliament. Our petitions have been slighted; our remonstrances have produced additional violence and insult; our supplications have been disregarded; and we have been spurned, with contempt, from the foot of the throne. In vain, after these things, may we indulge the fond hope of peace and reconciliation. *There is no longer any room for hope.* If we wish to be free—if we mean to preserve inviolate those inestimable privileges for which we have been so long contending—if we mean not basely to abandon the noble struggle in which we have been so long engaged, and which we have pledged ourselves never to abandon until the glorious object of our contest shall be obtained-we must fight! I repeat it, sir, we must fight!! An appeal to arms and to the God of Hosts, is all that is left us!' "

"'They tell us, sir, that we are weak-unable to cope with so formidable an adversary. But when shall we be stronger? Will it be the next week, or the next year? Will it be when we are totally disarmed, and when a British guard shall be stationed in every house? Shall we gather strength by irresolution and inaction? Shall we acquire the means of effectual resistance by lying supinely on our backs, and hugging the delusive phantom of Hope, until our enemies shall have bound us hand and foot? Sir, we are not weak, if we make a proper use of those means which the God of nature hath placed in our power. Three millions of people, armed in the holy cause of liberty, and in such a country as that which we possess, are invincible by any force which our enemy can send against us. Besides, sir, we shall not fight our battles alone. There is a just God who presides over the destinies of nations; and who will raise up friends to fight our battles for us. The battle, sir, is not to the strong alone; it is to the vigilant, the active, the brave. Besides, sir, we have no election. If we were base enough to desire it, it is now too late to retire from the contest. There is no retreat, but in submission and slavery! Our chains are forged, their clanking may be heard on the plains of Boston ! The war is inevitable-and let it come ! ! I repeat it, sir, let it come ! ! !

"'It is in vain sir, to extenuate the matter. Gentlemen may cry, peace, peace, but there is no peace. The war is actually begun ! The next gale that sweeps from the north will bring to our ears the clash of resounding arms ! Our brethren are already in the field! Why stand we here idle? What is it that gentlemen wish? What would they have? Is life so dear, or peace so sweet, as to be purchased at the price of chains and slavery? Forbid it, Almighty God ! I know not what course others may take; but as for me,' cried he, with both his arms extended aloft, his brows knit, every feature marked with the resolute purpose of his soul, and his voice swelled to its boldest note of exclamation—'give me liberty, or give me death!'"

7

CONFRONTATION AT HOLLYROOD

JOHN KNOX'S CONFRONTATION OF MARY
QUEEN OF SCOTS AT HOLLYROOD, SCOTLAND,
1561–1563

Source: C. J. Guthrie, Q.C., ed.; John Knox, *The History of the Reformation of Religion Within the Realm of Scotland* (The Banner of Truth Trust: Carlisle, PA, 1982; First edition 1898), 277–79, 316–17, 303–4.

(From First Meeting):

Queen Mary. "But yet ye have taught the people to receive another religion than their Princes can allow. How can that doctrine be of God, seeing that God commandeth subjects to obey their Princes? "

John Knox. "Madam, as right religion took neither original strength nor authority from worldly princes, but from the Eternal God alone, so are not subjects bound to frame their religion according to the appetites of their princes. Princes are oft the most ignorant of all others in God's true religion, as we may read in the Histories, as well before the birth of Christ Jesus as after. If all the seed of Abraham should have been of the religion of Pharaoh, to whom they were long subjects, I pray you, Madam, what religion should there have been in the world? Or, if all men in the days of the Apostles should have been of the religion of the Roman Emperors, what religion should there have been upon the face of the earth? Daniel and his fellows were subject to Nebuchadnezzar and unto Darius, and yet, Madam, they would not be of their religion; for the three children said: 'We make it known unto thee, O King, that we will not worship thy Gods.' Daniel did pray publicly unto his God against the expressed commandment of the King. And so, Madam, ye may perceive that subjects are not bound to the religion of their princes, although they are commanded to give them obedience."

Queen Mary. "Yea, but none of these men raised the sword against their princes."

John Knox. "Yet, Madam, ye can not deny that they resisted, for those who obey not the commandments that are given, in some sort resist."

Queen Mary. "But yet, they resisted not by the sword?"

John Knox. "God, Madam, had not given them the power and the means."

Queen Mary. "Think ye that subjects, having the power, may resist their princes?"

John Knox. "If their princes exceed their bounds, Madam, no doubt they may be resisted, even by power. For there is neither greater honour, nor greater obedience, to be given to kings or princes, than God hath commanded to be given unto father and mother. But the father may be stricken with a frenzy, in which he would slay his children. If the children arise, join themselves together, apprehend the father, take the sword from him, bind his hands, and keep him in prison till his frenzy be overpast— think ye, Madam, that the children do any wrong? It is even so, Madam, with princes that would murder the children of God that are subjects unto them. Their blind zeal is nothing but a very mad frenzy, and therefore, to take the sword from them, to bind their hands, and to cast them into prison, till they be brought to a more sober mind, is no disobedience against princes, but just obedience, because it agreeth with the will of God."

Queen Mary. "Well then, I perceive that my subjects shall obey you, and and not me. They shall do what they list, and not what I command; and so must I be subject to them, and not they to me."

John Knox. "God forbid that ever I take upon me to command any to obey me, or yet to set subjects at liberty to do what pleaseth them! My travail is that both princes and subjects obey God. Think not, Madam, that wrong is done you, when ye are willed to be subject to God. It is He that subjects peoples under princes, and causes obedience to be given unto them. Yea, God craves of Kings that they be foster-fathers to His Church, and commands Queens to be nurses to His people. This subjection, Madam, unto God, and unto His troubled Church, is the greatest dignity that flesh can get upon the face of the earth; for it shall carry them to everlasting glory."

(From Second Interview):

"After, Madam, I had declared the dignity of kings, the honour wherein God hath placed them, and the obedience that is due unto them, being God's Lieutenants, I demanded this question: What account shall most Princes make before that Supreme Judge, whose authority so shamefully they abuse? Whilst murderers, oppressors, and malefactors dare be bold to present themselves before Kings, whilst the poor saints of God are banished, what shall we say, but that the Devil hath taken possession in the Throne of God, which ought to be fearful to all wicked doers, and a refuge to the innocent oppressed. How can it otherwise be? Princes despise God's law; His statues and holy ordinances they will not understand. In fiddling and flinging [dancing] they are more exercised than in reading or hearing God's Most Blessed Word; and fiddlers and flatterers are more precious in their eyes than men of wisdom and gravity, who by wholesome admonition might beat down in them some part of that pride wherein we all are born, but which in Princes taketh deep root by wicked education."

(From Third Interview):

"Will ye, " quoth she, "allow that they shall take *my* sword in their hand?'

"The Sword of Justice," quoth he, "Madam, is *God's*, and is given to princes and rulers for one end, which if they transgress, sparing the wicked and oppressing innocents, their subjects, who in the fear of God execute judgment, where God hath commanded, offend not God, neither do they sin that bridle Kings from striking innocent men in their rage. The examples are evident:-Samuel feared not to slay Agag, the fat and delicate King of Amalek, whom King Saul had saved. . . . It shall be profitable to Your Majesty to consider what is the thing Your Grace's subjects look to receive of Your Majesty, and what it is that ye ought to do unto them by mutual contract. They are bound to obey you, and that not but in God: ye are bound to keep laws unto them. Ye crave of them service; they crave of you protection and defence against wicked doers. Now, Madam, if you shall deny your duty unto them, who especially crave that ye punish malefactors, think ye to receive full obedience from them? I fear, Madam, ye shall not."

8

CROMWELL VS. CHARLES I

OLIVER CROMWELL'S DEATH WARRANT FOR CHARLES I, ENGLAND, 1649

Source: J. H. Merle D'Aubigne, D.D., *The Protector: A Vindication.* (Harrisonburg, VA: Sprinkle Publications, 1993), 77–79.
Samuel Rawson Gardiner, ed., *The Constitutional Documents of the Puritan Revolution 1628–1660* (Oxford: At the Clarendon Press, 1889), 282–90.

"We met at Windsor Castle about the beginning of Forty-eight, and there we spent one day together in prayer; inquiring into the causes of that sad dispensation;coming to no further resolve that day;but that it was still our duty to seek. And on the morrow we met again in the morning, where many spake from the Word and prayed; and the then Lieutenant-General Cromwell did press very earnestly on all there present to a thorough consideration of our actions as an army, and of our ways, particularly as private Christians: to see if any iniquity could be found in them, and what it was; that if possible we might find it out, and so remove the cause of such sad rebukes as were upon us at that time. And to this end," he added, "let us consider when we could last say that the presence of the Lord was among us, and rebukes and judgments were not as then upon us. We concluded this second day with agreeing to meet again on the morrow."

"Which accordingly we did, and were led by a gracious hand of the Lord, to find out the very steps by which we had departed from Him, and provoked Him to depart from us. Which we found to be those cursed carnal conferences our own conceited wisdom, our fears, and want of faith had prompted us, the year before, to entertain with the King and his party. And on this occasion did the then Major Goffe make use of that good Word, Proverbs 1:23: *Turn you at my reproof: behold, I will pour out my spirit unto you, I will make known my words unto you.* And the Lord so accompanied this invitation by His Spirit, that it had a kindly effect, like a word of His, upon most of our hearts that were then present; which begot in us a great sense, a shame and loathing of ourselves for our iniquities, and a justifying of the Lord as righteous in His proceedings against us. He led us not only to see our sin, but also our duty; and this so unanimously set with weight upon each heart, that none was able hardly to speak a word to each other for bitter weeping, partly in the sense and shame of our iniquities; of our unbelief, base fear of men, and carnal consultations with our own wisdom, and not with the Word of the Lord. . . . And yet we were also helped, with fear and trembling, to rejoice in the Lord, who no sooner brought us to His feet but He did direct our steps, and we were led to a clear agreement amongst ourselves, that it was the duty of our day, with the forces we had, to go out and fight against our potent enemies, with an humble confidence in the name of the Lord only.

"And we were also enabled then, after serious seeking the Lord's face, to come to a very clear and joint resolution, that it was our duty to call Charles Stuart, that man of blood, to an account for that blood he had shed, and mischief he had done to his utmost against the Lord's cause and people in these poor nations."*

*Somer's Tracts, vi.499–501; cited by Carlyle, i.337–340.

72. The Charge Against The King.

[January 20, 164, Rushworth, vii. 1396. See Masson's *Life of Milton*, iii. 708.]
That the said Charles Stuart, being admitted King of England, and therein trusted with a limited power to govern by, and according to the laws of the land, and not otherwise; and by his trust, oath, and office, being obliged to use the power committed to him for the good and benefit of the people, and for the preserva-

tion of their rights and liberties; yet, nevertheless, out of a wicked design to erect and uphold in himself an unlimited and tyrannical power to rule according to his will, and to overthrow the rights and liberties of the people, yea, to take away and make void the foundations thereof, and of all redress and remedy of misgovernment, which by the fundamental constitutions of this kingdom were reserved on the peoples' behalf in the right and power of frequent and successive Parliaments, or national meetings in Council; he, the said Charles Stuart, for accomplishment of such his designs, and for the protecting of himself and his adherents in his and their wicked practices, to the same ends hath traitorously and maliciously levied war against the present Parliament, and the people therein represented, particularly upon or about the 30th day of June, in the year of our Lord 1642, at Beverley, in the County of York; and upon or about the 24th day of August in the same year, at the County of the Town of Nottingham, where and when he set up his standard of war; and also on or about the 23rd day of October in the same year, at Edgehill or Keyntonfield, in the County of Warwick; and upon or about the 30th day of November in the same year, at Brentford, in the County of Middlesex; and upon or about the 30th day of August, in the year of our Lord 1643, at the Caversham Bridge, near Reading, in the County of Berks; and upon or about the 30th day of October in the year last mentioned, at or upon the City of Gloucester; and upon or about the 30th day of November in the year last mentioned, at Newbury, in the County of Berks; and upon or about the 31st day of July, in the year of our Lord 1644, at Cropredy Bridge, in the County of Oxon; and upon or about the 30th day of September in the last year mentioned, at Bodmin and other places near adjacent, in the County of Cornwall; and upon or about the 30th day of November in the year last mentioned, at Newbury aforesaid; and upon or about the 8th day of June, in the year of our Lord 1645, at the Town of Leicester; and also upon the 14th day of the same month in the same year, at Naseby-field, in the County of North-ampton. At which several times and places, or most of them, and at many other places in this land, at several other times within the years aforementioned, and in the year of our Lord 1646, he, the said Charles Stuart, hath caused and procured many thousands of the free people of this nation to be slain; and by divisions, parties, and insurrections within this land, by invasions from foreign parts, endeavoured and procured by him, and by many other evil ways and means, he, the said Charles Stuart, hath not only maintained and carried on the said war both by land and sea, during the years beforementioned, but also hath renewed, or caused to be renewed, the said war against the Parliament and good people of this nation in this present year 1648, in the Counties of Kent, Essex, Surrey, Sussex, Middlesex, and many other Counties and places in England and Wales, and also by sea. And particularly he, the said Charles Stuart, hath for that purpose given commission to his son the Prince, and others, whereby, besides multitudes of other persons, many such as were by the Parliament entrusted and employed for the safety of the nation (being by him or his agents corrupted to the betraying of their trust, and revolting from the Parliament), have had entertainment and commission for the continuing and renewing of war and hostility against the said Parliament and people as aforesaid. By which cruel and unnatural wars, by him, the said Charles Stuart, levied, continued, and renewed as aforesaid, much innocent blood of the free people of this nation hath been spilt, many families have been undone, the public treasure wasted and exhausted, trade obstructed and miserably decayed, vast expense and damage to the nation incurred, and many parts of this land spoiled, some of them even to desolation. And for further prosecution of his said evil designs, he, the said Charles Stuart, doth still continue his commissions to the said Prince, and other rebels and revolters, both English and foreigners, and to the Earl of Ormond, and the Irish rebels and revolters associated with him; from whom further invasions upon this land are threatened, upon the procurement, and on the behalf of the said Charles Stuart.

All which wicked designs, wars, and evil practices of him, the said Charles Stuart, have been, and are carried on for the advancement and upholding of a personal interest of will, power, and pretended prerogative to himself and his family, against the public interest, common right, liberty, justice, and peace of the people of this nation, by and from whom he was entrusted as aforesaid.

By all which it appeareth that the said Charles Stuart hath been, and is the occasioner, author, and continuer of the said unnatural, cruel and bloody wars; and therein guilty of all the treasons, murders, rapines, burnings, spoils, desolations, damages, and mischiefs to this nation, acted and committed in the said wars, or occasioned thereby.

73. The King's Reasons For Declining The Jurisdiction Of The High Court Of Justice.

[January 21, 164, Rushworth, vii. 1403.]

Having already made my protestations, not only against the illegality of this pretended Court, but also, that no earthly power can justly call me (who am your King) in question as a delinquent, I would not any more open my mouth upon this occasion, more than to refer myself to what I have spoken, were I in this case alone concerned: but the duty I owe to God in the preservation of the true liberty of my people will not suffer me at this time to be silent: for, how can any free-born subject of England call life or anything he possesseth his own, if power without right daily make new, and abrogate the old fundamental laws of the land which I now take to be the present case? Wherefore when I came hither, I expected that you would have endeavoured to have satisfied me concerning these grounds which hinder me to answer to your pretended impeachment. But since I see that nothing I can say will move you to it (though negatives are not so naturally proved as affirmatives) yet I will show you the reason why I am confident you cannot judge me, nor indeed the meanest man in England: for I will not (like you) without shewing a reason, seek to impose a belief upon my subjects.

There is no proceeding just against any man, but what is warranted, either by God's laws or the municipal laws of the country where he lives. Now I am most confident this day's proceeding cannot be warranted by God's laws; for, on the contrary, the authority of obedience unto Kings is clearly warranted, and strictly commanded in both the Old and New Testament, which, if denied, I am ready instantly to prove.

And for the question now in hand, there it is said, that 'where the word of a King is, there is power; and who may say unto him, what dost thou? ' Eccles. viii. Then for the law of this land, I am no less confident, that no learned lawyer will affirm that an impeachment can lie against the King, they all going in his name: and one of their maxims is, that the King can do no wrong. Besides, the law upon which you ground your proceedings, must either be old or new: if old, show it; if new, tell what authority, warranted by the fundamental laws of the land, hath made it, and when. But how the House of Commons can erect a Court of Judicature, which was never one itself (as is well known to all lawyers) I leave to God and the world to judge. And it were full as strange, that they should pretend to make laws without King or Lords' House, to any that have heard speak of the laws of England.

And admitting, but not granting, that the people of England's commission could grant your pretended power, I see nothing you can show for that; for certainly you never asked the question of the tenth man in the kingdom, and in this way you manifestly wrong even the poorest ploughman, if you demand not his free consent: nor can you pretend any colour for this your pretended commission, without the consent at least of the major part of every man in England of whatsoever quality or condition, which I am sure you never went about to seek, so far are from having it. Thus you see that I speak not for my own right alone, as I am your King, but also for the true liberty of all my subjects, which consists not in the power of government, but in living under such laws, such a government, as may give themselves the best assurance of their lives, and property of their goods; nor in this must or do I forget the privileges of both Houses of Parliament, which this day's proceedings do not only violate, but likewise occasion the greatest breach of their public faith that (I believe) ever was heard of, with which I am far from charging the two Houses; for all the pretended crimes laid against me bear date long before this Treaty at Newport, in which I having concluded as much as in me lay, and hopefully expecting the Houses' agreement thereunto, I was suddenly surprised and hurried from thence as a prisoner; upon which account I am against my will brought hither, where since I am come, I cannot but to my power defend the ancient laws and liberties of this kingdom, together with my own just right. Then for anything I can see, the higher House is totally excluded; and for the House of Commons, it is too well known that the major part of them are detained or deterred from sitting; so as if I had no other, this were sufficient for me to protest against the lawfulness of your pretended Court. Besides all this, the peace of the kingdom is not the least in my thoughts;

and what hope of settlement is there, so long as power reigns without rule or law, changing the whole frame of that government under which this kingdom hath flourished for many hundred years? (nor will I say what will fall out in case this lawless, unjust proceeding against me do go on) and believe it, the Commons of England will not thank you for this change; for they will remember how happy they have been of late years under the reigns of Queen Elizabeth, the King my father, and myself, until the beginning of these unhappy troubles, and will have cause to doubt, that they shall never be so happy under any new: and by this time it will be too sensibly evident, that the arms I took up were only to defend the fundamental laws of this kingdom against those who have supposed my power hath totally changed the ancient government.

Thus, having shewed you briefly the reasons why I cannot submit to your pretended authority, without violating the trust which I have from God for the welfare and liberty of my people, I expect from you either clear reasons to convince my judgment, shewing me that I am in an error (and then truly I will answer) or that you will withdraw your proceedings.

This I intended to speak in Westminster Hall, on Monday, January 22, but against reason was hindered to show my reasons.

74. The Sentence Of The High Court Of Justice Upon The King.

[January 27, 1649. Rushworth, viii. 1420. See Masson's Life of Milton, iii., 711]

Whereas the Commons of England assembled in Parliament, have by their late Act intituled an Act of the Commons of England assembled in Parliament, for erecting an High Court of Justice for the trying and judging of Charles Stuart, King of England, authorised and constituted us an High Court of Justice for the trying and judging of the said Charles Stuart for the crimes and treasons in the said Act mentioned; by virtue whereof the said Charles Stuart hath been three several times convented before this High Court, where the first day, being Saturday, the 20th of January, instant, in pursuance of the said Act, a charge of high treason and other high crimes was, in the behalf of the people of England, exhibited against him, and read openly unto him, wherein he was charged, that he, the said Charles Stuart, being admitted King of England, and therein trusted with a limited power to govern by, and according to the law of the land, and not otherwise; and by his trust, oath, and office, being obliged to use the power committed to him for the good and benefit of the people, and for the preservation of their rights and liberties; yet, nevertheless, out of a wicked design to erect and uphold in himself an unlimited and tyrannical power to rule according to his will, and to overthrow the rights and liberties of the people, and to take away and make void the foundations thereof, and of all redress and remedy of misgovernment, which by the fundamental constitutions of this kingdom were reserved on the peoples' behalf in the right and power of frequent and successive Parliaments, or national meetings in Council; he, the said Charles Stuart, for accomplishment of such his designs, and for the protecting of himself and his adherents in his and their wicked practices, to the same end hath traitorously and maliciously levied war against the present Parliament, and people therein represented, as with the circumstances of time and place is in the said charge more particularly set forth; and that he hath thereby caused and procured many thousands of the free people of this nation to be slain; and by divisions, parties, and insurrections within this land, by invasions from foreign parts, endeavoured and procured by him, and by many other evil ways and means, he, the said Charles Stuart, hath not only maintained and carried on the said war both by sea and land, but also hath renewed, or caused to be renewed, the said war against the Parliament and good people of this nation in this present year 1648, in several counties and places in this kingdom in the charge specified; and that he hath for that purpose given his commission to his son the Prince, and others, whereby, besides multitudes of other persons, many such as were by the Parliament entrusted and employed for the safety of this nation, being by him or his agents corrupted to the betraying of their trust, and revolting from the Parliament, have had entertainment and commission for the continuing and renewing of the war and hostility against the said Parliament and people: and that by the said cruel and unnatural war so levied, continued and renewed, much innocent blood of the free people of this nation hath been spilt, many families undone, the public treasure wasted, trade obstructed and miserably decayed, vast expense and damage to the nation incurred, and many parts of the land spoiled, some of them even to desolation; and that he still continues his commission to his said son, and other rebels and revolters, both English and foreigners, and to the Earl of Ormond, and to the Irish rebels and revolters associated with him, from whom further invasions of this land are threatened by his procurement and on his behalf; and that all the said wicked designs, wars, and evil practices of him, the said Charles Stuart, were still carried on for the advancement and upholding of the personal interest of will, power, and pretended prerogative to himself and his family, against the public interest, common right, liberty, justice, and peace of the people of this nation; and that he thereby hath been and is the occasioner, author, and continuer of the said unnatural, cruel, and bloody wars, and therein guilty of all the treasons, murders, rapines, burnings, spoils, desolations, damage, and mischief to this nation, acted and committed in the said wars, or occasioned thereby; whereupon the proceedings and judgment of this Court were prayed against him, as a tyrant, traitor, and murderer, and public enemy to the Commonwealth, as by the said charge more fully appeareth. To which charge, being read unto him as aforesaid, he, the said Charles Stuart, was required to give his answer; but he refused so to do, and upon Monday, the 22nd day of January instant, being again brought before this Court, and there required to answer directly to the said charge, he still refused so to do; whereupon his default and contumacy was entered; and the next day, being the third time brought before the Court, judgment was then prayed against him on the behalf of the people of England for his contumacy, and for the matters contained against him in the said charge, as taking the same for confessed, in regard of his refusing to answer thereto: yet notwithstanding this Court (not willing to take advantage of his contempt) did once more require him to answer to the said charge; but he again refused so to do; upon which his several defaults, this Court might justly have proceeded to judgment against him, both for his contumacy and the matters of the charge, taking the same for confessed as aforesaid.

Yet nevertheless this Court, for its own clearer information and further satisfaction, have thought fit to examine witnesses upon oath, and take notice of other evidences, touching the matters contained in the said charge, which accordingly they have done.

Now, therefore, upon serious and mature deliberation of the premises, and consideration had of the notoriety of the matters of fact charged upon him as aforesaid, this Court is in judgment and conscience satisfied that he, the said Charles Stuart, is guilty of levying war against the said Parliament and people, and maintaining and continuing the same; for which in the said charge he stands accused, and by the general course of his government, counsels, and practices, before and since this Parliament began (which have been and are notorious and public, and the effects whereof remain abundantly upon record) this Court is fully satisfied in their judgments and consciences, that he has been and is guilty of the wicked designs and endeavours in the said charge set forth; and that the said war hath been levied, maintained, and continued by him as aforesaid, in prosecution, and for accomplishment of the said designs; and that he hath been and is the occasioner, author, and continuer of the said unnatural, cruel, and bloody wars, and therein guilty of high treason, and of the murders, rapines, burnings, spoils, desolations, damage, and mischief to this nation acted and committed in the said war, and occasioned thereby. For all which treasons and crimes this Court doth adjudge that he, the said Charles Stuart, as a tyrant, traitor, murderer, and public enemy to the good people of this nation, shall be put to death by the severing of his head from his body.

75. The Death Warrant Of Charles I.

[January 29, 164, Rushworth, vii. 1426. See Masson's *Life of Milton*, iii. 719.]

At the High Court of Justice for the trying and judging of Charles Stuart, King of England, Jan. 29, Anno Domini 1648.

Whereas Charles Stuart, King of England, is, and standeth convicted, attainted, and condemned of high treason, and other high crimes; and sentence upon Saturday last was pronounced against him by this Court, to be put to death by the severing of his head from his body; of which sentence, execution yet remaineth to be done; these are therefore to will and require you to see the said sentence executed in the open street before Whitehall, upon the morrow, being the thirtieth day of this instant month of January, between the hours of ten in the morning and five in the afternoon of the same day, with full effect. And for so doing this shall be your sufficient warrant. And these are to require all officers, soldiers, and others, the good people of this nation of England, to be assisting unto you in this service.

To Col. Francis Hacker, Col. Huncks, and Lieut.-Col. Phayre, and to every of them.

Given under our hands and seals.

John Bradshaw
Thomas Grey
Oliver Cromwell
&c. &c.

9

INDEPENDENCE DAY

THE DECLARATION OF INDEPENDENCE
(JULY 4, 1776)

For Further Study, see: Gary T. Amos, *Defending The Declaration* (Brentwood, TN: Wolgemuth & Hyatt, Publishers, Inc., 1989), 171–75.

The Unanimous Declaration of the Thirteen United States of America

When, in the course of human events, it becomes necessary for one people to dissolve the political bands which have connected them with another, and to assume, among the powers of the earth, the separate and equal station to which the laws of nature and of nature's God entitle them, a decent respect to the opinions of mankind requires that they should declare the causes which impels them to the separation.

We hold these truths to be self-evident: that all men are created equal; that they are endowed, by their Creator, with certain unalienable rights; that among these are life, liberty, and the pursuit of happiness. That to secure these rights, governments are instituted among men, deriving their just powers from the consent of the governed; that whenever any form of government becomes destructive of these ends, it is the right of the people to alter or to abolish it, and to institute a new government, laying its foundation on such principles, and organizing its powers in such form, as to them shall seem most likely to effect their safety and happiness. Prudence, indeed, will dictate, that governments long established, should not be changed for light and transient causes; and accordingly all experience hath shown, that mankind are more disposed to suffer, while evils are sufferable, than to right themselves by abolishing the forms to which they are accustomed. But when a long train of abuses and usurpations, pursuing invariably the same object, evinces a design to reduce them under absolute despotism, it is their right, it is their duty, to throw off such government, and to provide new guards for their future security. Such has been the patient sufferance of these colonies; and such is now the necessity which constrains them to alter their former systems of government. The history of the present King of Great Britain is a history of repeated injuries and usurpations, all having in direct object the establishment of an absolute tyranny over these states. To prove this, let facts be submitted to a candid world.

He has refused his assent to laws the most wholesome and necessary for the public good.

He has forbidden his governors to pass laws of immediate and pressing importance, unless suspended in their operation till his assent should be obtained; and when so suspended, he has utterly neglected to attend to them.

He has refused to pass other laws for the accommodation of the large districts of people, unless those people would relinquish the right of representation in the legislature; a right inestimable to them, and formidable to tyrants only. He has called together legislative bodies at places unusual, uncomfortable, and distant from the depository of their public records, for the sole purpose of fatiguing them into compliance with his measures.

He has dissolved representative houses repeatedly, for opposing, with manly firmness, his invasions on the rights of the people.

He has refused for a long time, after such dissolutions, to cause others to be elected; whereby the legislative powers, incapable of annihilation, have returned to the people at large for their exercise; the state remaining, in the mean time, exposed to all the dangers of invasions from without, and convulsions within.

He has endeavored to prevent the population of these States; for that purpose obstructing the laws for naturalization of foreigners; refusing to pass others to encourage their migrations hither, and raising the conditions of new appropriations of lands.

He has made judges dependent on his will alone, for the tenure of their offices, and the amount and payment of their salaries.

He has erected a multitude of new offices, and sent hither swarms of officers, to harass our people, and eat out their substance.

He has kept among us, in times of peace, standing armies, without the consent of our legislatures.

He has affected to render the military independent of, and superior to the civil power.

He has combined with others to subject us to a jurisdiction foreign to our constitution, and unacknowledged by our laws; giving his assent to their acts of pretended legislation:

For quartering large bodies of armed troops among us;

For protecting them, by a mock trial, from punishment for any murders which they should commit on the inhabitants of these States;

For cutting off our trade with all parts of the world;

For imposing taxes on us with out our consent;

For depriving us, in many cases, of the benefits of trial by jury;

For transporting us beyond seas to be tried for pretended offences; For abolishing the free system of English laws in a neighbouring province, establishing therein an arbitrary government, and enlarging its boundaries, so as to render it as once an example and fit instrument for introducing the same absolute rule into these colonies;

For taking away our charters, abolishing our most valuable laws, and altering fundamentally the forms of our governments;

For suspending our own legislatures, and declaring themselves invested with power to legislate for us in all cases whatsoever.

He has abdicated government here, by declaring us out of his protection, and waging war against us.

He has plundered our seas, ravaged our coasts, burnt our towns, and destroyed the lives of our people.

He is at this time transporting large armies of foreign mercenaries to complete the works of death, desolation, and tyranny, already begun with circumstances of cruelty and perfidy, scarcely paralleled in the most barbarous ages, and totally unworthy the head of a civilized nation.

He has constrained our fellow-citizens, taken captive on the high seas, to bear arms against their country, to become the executioners of their friends and brethren, or to fall themselves by their hands.

He has excited domestic insurrections amongst us, and has endeavoured to bring on the inhabitants of our frontiers the merciless Indian savages, whose known rule of warfare is an undistinguished destruction of all ages, sexes, and conditions.

In every stage of these oppressions we have petitioned for redress in the most humble terms. Our repeated petitions have been answered only by repeated injury. A prince, whose character is thus marked by every act which may define a tyrant, is unfit to be the ruler of a free people.

Nor have we been wanting in attentions to our British brethren. We have warned them, from time to time, of attempts by their legislature to extend an unwarrantable jurisdiction over us. We have reminded them of the circumstances of our emigration and settlement here. We have appealed to their native justice and magnanimity, and we have conjured them by the ties of our common kindred to disavow these usurpations, which would inevitably interrupt our connexions and correspondence. They too have been deaf to the voice of justice and of consanguinity. We must, therefore, acquiesce in the necessity which denounces our separation, and hold them, as we hold the rest of mankind, enemies in war, in peace friends.

We, therefore, the representatives of the United States of America, in General Congress assembled, appealing to the Supreme Judge of the world for the rectitude of our intentions, do, in the name, and by authority of the good people of these colonies, solemnly publish and declare, That these United Colonies are, and of right ought to be, Free and Independent States; that they are absolved from all allegiance, to the British crown, and that all political connexion between them and the state of Great Britian is, and ought to be, totally dissolved; and that, as Free and Independent States, they have full power to levy war, conclude peace, contract alliances, establish commerce, and to do all other acts and thing which Independent States may of right do. And for the support of Declaration, with a firm reliance on the protection of Divine Providence, we mutually pledge to each other our lives, our fortunes, and our sacred honour.

John Hancock, et al.

10

THE LAW AND THE PRINCE

SAMUEL RUTHERFORD'S LEX, REX, OR THE LAW AND THE PRINCE

Source: Rev. Samuel Rutherford, *Lex, Rex, or The Law and the Prince* (Harrisonburg, VA:Sprinkle Publications, 1982—original London:John Field, October 7, 1644), 117–18, 139, 141–42, 145, 149.

Ans. ..2. Tyranny is more visible and intelligible than heresy, and is soon decerned. If a king bring in upon his native subjects twenty thousand Turks armed, and the king lead them, it is evident they come not to make a friendly visit to salute the kingdom, and depart in peace. The people have a natural throne of policy in their conscience to give warning and materially sentence against the king as a tyrant, and so by nature are to defend themselves. Where tyranny is more obscure, and the thread small, that it escape the eye of men, the king keepeth possession; but I deny that tyranny can be obscure long. . . .

Obj. 4.-An absolute monarch is free from all forcible restraint, and so far as he is absolute from all legal restraints of positive laws. Now, in a limited monarch, there is only sough a legal restraint; and limitation cannot infer a forcible restraint, for an absolute monarch is limited also, not by civil compact, but by the law of nature and nations, which he cannot justly transgress. If therefore an absolute monarch, being exorbitant, may not be resisted because he transgresseth the law of nature, how shall we think a limited monarch may be resisted for transgressing the bounds set by civil agreement.

Ans. 1.-A legal restraint on the people is a forcible restraint; for if law be not backed with force, it is only a law of rewarding well-doing, which is no restraint, but an encouragement to do evil. If, then, there be a legal restraint upon the king, without any force, it is not restraint, but only such a request as this: be a just prince, and we will give your majesty two subsidies in one year. 2. I utterly deny that God ever ordained such an irrational creature as an absolute monarch. If a people unjustly, and against nature's dictates, make away irrevocably their own liberty, and the liberty of their posterity, which is not their's to dispose off, and set over themselves as base slaves, a sinning creature, with absolute power, he is their king, but not as he is absolute, and that he may not be forcibly resisted, notwithstanding the subjects did swear to his absolute power, (which oath in the point of absoluteness is unlawful, and so not obligatory,) I utterly deny. 3. An absolute monarch (saith he) is limited, but by law of nature. That is Master Doctor, he is not limited as a monarch, not as an absolute monarch, but as a son of Adam; he is under the limits of the law of nature, which he should have been under though he had never been a king all his days, but a slave. But what then? Therefore, he cannot be resisted. Yes, Doctor, by your own grant he can be resisted: if he invade an innocent subject (say you) suddenly, without colour of law, or inevitably; and that because he transgresseth the law of nature. You say a limited monarch can less be resisted for transgressing the bounds set by civil agreement. But what if the thus limited monarch transgress the law of nature, and subvert fundamental laws? He is then, you seem to say, to be resisted. It is not for simple transgression of a civil agreement that he is to be resisted. The limited monarch is an essentially the Lord's anointed, and the power ordained of God, as the absolute monarch. Now resistance by all your grounds is unlawful, because of God's power and place conferred upon him, not because of men's positive covenant made with him. . . .

QUESTION XXVIII.

Whether or no wars raised by the subject and estates, for their own just defence against the king's bloody emissaries, be lawful.

For the lawfulness of resistance in the matter of the king's unjust invasion of life and religion, we offer these arguments.

Arg. 1. That power which is obliged to command and rule justly and religiously for the good of the subjects, and is only set over the people on these conditions, and not absolutely, cannot tie the people to subjection without resistance, when the power is abused to the destruction of laws, religion, and the subjects. But all power of the law is thus obliged, (Rom. xiii. 4; Deut. xvii. 18–20; 2 Chron. xix.6; Ps. cxxxii. 11, 12; lxxxix.30,31; 2 Sam. vii.12; Jer. xvii. 24,25,) and hath, and may be, abused by kings, to the destruction of laws, religion, and subjects. The proposition is clear. 1. For the power that tie us to subjection only are of God. 2. Because to resist them, is to resist the ordinance of God. 3. Because they are not a terror to good works, but to evil. 4. Because they are God's ministers for our good, but abused powers are not of God, but of men, or not ordinances of God; they are a terror to good works, not to evil; they are not God's ministers for our good.

Arg. 2. That power which is contrary to law, and is evil and tyrannical, can tie none to subjection, but is a mere tyrannical power and unlawful; and if it tie not to subjection, it may lawfully be resisted. But the power of the king, abused to the destruction of laws, religion, and subjects, is a power contrary to law, evil, and tyrannical, and tyeth no man to subjection: wickedness by no imaginable reason can oblige any man. Obligation to suffer of wicked men falleth under no commandment of God, except in our Saviour. A passion, as such, is not formally commanded, I mean a physical passion, such as to be killed. God hath not said to me in any moral law, Be thou killed, tortured, beheaded; but only Be thou patient, if God deliver thee to wicked men's hands, to suffer these things.

Arg. 3. There is not a stricter obligation moral betwixt king and people than betwixt parents and children, master and servant, patron and clients, husband and wife, the lord and the vassal, between the pilot of a ship and the passengers, the physician and the sick, the doctor and the scholars, but the law granteth, (*l. Minime* 35, *de Relig. et sumpt. funer,*) if these betray their trust committed to them, they may be resisted: if the father turn distracted, and arise to kill his sons, his sons may violently apprehend him, and bind his hands, and spoil him of his weapons; for in that he is not a father. . . The servant may resist the master if he attempts unjustly to kill him, so may the wife do to the husband; if the pilot should wilfully run the ship on a rock to destroy himself and his passengers, they might violently thrust him from the helm. Every tyrant is a furious man, and is morally distracted, as Althusius saith, Polit. c. 28,n.30, and seq.

Arg. 4. That which is given as a blessing, and a favour, and a screen, between the people's liberty and their bondage, cannot be given of God as a bondage and slavery to the people. But the power of a king is given as a blessing and favour of God to defend the poor and needy, to preserve both tables of the law, and to keep the people in their liberties from oppressing and treading one upon another. But so it, that if such a power be given of God to a king, by which, *actu primo*, he is invested of God to do acts of tyranny, and so to do them, that to resist him in the most innocent way, which is self-defence, must be a resisting of God, and rebellion against the king, his deputy; then hath God given a royal power as uncontrollable by mortal men, by any violence, as if God himself were immediately and personally resisted, when the king is resisted, and so this power shall be a power to waste and destroy irresistibly, and so in itself a plague and a curse; for it cannot be ordained both according to the intention and genuine formal effect and intrinsical operation of the power, to preserve the tables of the law, religion and liberty, subjects and laws, and also to destroy the same. But it is taught by royalists that this power is for tyranny, as well as for peaceable government; because to resist this royal power put forth in acts either ways, either in acts of tyranny or just government, is to resist the ordinance of God, as royalists say, from Rom. xiii. 1–3. And we know, to resist God's ordinances and God's deputy, formaliter, as his deputy, is to resist God himself, (1 Sam. viii. 7; Matt. x. 40,) as if God were doing personally these acts that the king is doing; and it importeth as much as the King of kings doth these acts in and through the tyrant. Now, it is blasphemy to think or say, that when a king is drinking the blood of innocents, and wasting the church of God, that God, if he were personally present, would commit these same acts of tyranny, (God avert such blasphemy!) and that God in and through the king, as his lawful deputy and vicegerent in these acts of tyranny, is wasting the poor church of God. If it be said, in these sinful acts of tyranny, he is not God's formal vicegerent, but only in good and lawful acts of government, yet he is not to be resisted in these acts, not because the acts are just and good, but because of the dignity of his royal person. Yet this just prove that those who resist the king in these acts of tyranny, must resist no ordinance of God, but only resist him who is the Lord's deputy, though not as the Lord's deputy. What absurdity is there in that more than to disobey him, refusing active obedience to him who is the Lord's deputy, not as the Lord's deputy, but as a man commanding besides his master's warrant?. . . .

QUESTION XXIX.

Whether, in the case of defensive war, the distinction of the person of the king, as a man, who can commit acts of hostile tyranny against his subjects, and of the office and royal power that he hath from god and the people, as a king, can have place.

5. The lawful ruler, as a ruler, and in respect of his office, is not be resisted, because he is not a terror to good works, but to evil; and no man who doth good is to be afraid of the office or the power, but to expect praise and a reward of the same. But the man who is a king may command an idolatrous and superstitious worship-send an army of cut-throats against them, . . . and may imprison, deprive, confine, cut the ears, and slit the noses, and burn the faces of those who speak and preach and write the truth of God; and may send armies of cut-throats, Irish rebels, and other papists and malignant atheists, to destroy and murder the judges of the land, and innocent defenders of

the reformed religion, the man, I say, in these acts is
a terror to good works,-an encouragement to evil;
and those that do good are to be afraid of the king,
and to expect no praise, but punishment and vexation
from him; therefore, this reason in the text will prove
that the man who is the king, in so far as he doth those
things that are against his office, may be resisted; and
that in these we are not to subject, but only we are to
be subject to his power and royal authority, *in abstracto*, in so far as, according to his office, he is not a
terror to good works, but to evil.

6. The lawful ruler is the minister of God, or the
servant of God, for good to the commonwealth; and
to resist the servant in that wherein he is a servant,
and using the power that he hath from his master, is
to resist the Lord his master. But the man who is the
king, commanding unjust things, and killing the innocent, in these acts is not the minister of God for the
good of the commonwealth; he serveth himself, and
papists, and prelates, for the destruction of religion,
laws, and commonwealth: therefore the man may be
resisted; by this text when the office and power cannot be resisted.

7. The ruler, as the ruler, and the nature and
intrinsical end of the office is, that he bear God's
sword as an avenger to execute wrath on him that
doth evil, and so cannot be resisted without sin. But
the man who is the ruler, and commandeth things
unlawful, and killeth the innocent, carrieth the pa-
pist's and prelate's sword to execute, not the righteous judgment of the Lord upon the ill-doer, but his
own private revenge upon him that doth well; there-

fore, the man may be resisted, the office may not be resisted; and they must be two different things.

8. We must needs be subject to the royal office for conscience, by reason of the fifth commandment; but we must no needs be subject to the man who is king, if he command things unlawful; for Dr Ferne warranteth us to resist, if the ruler invade us suddenly, without colour of law or reason, and unavoidably; and Winzetus, Barclay, and Grotius, as before I cited, give us leave to resist a king turning a cruel tyrant; but Paul (Rom. xiii.) forbiddeth us to resist the power, *in abstracto*; therefore, it must be the man, *in concreto*, that we must resist.

9. Those we may not resist to whom we owe tribute, as a reward of the onerous work on which they, as ministers of God, do attend continually. But we owe not tribute to the king as a man,-for then should we be indebted tribute to all men,-but as a king, to whom the wages of tribute is due, as to a princely workman,- a king as a king;-therefore, the man and the king are different.

10. We owe fear and honour as due to be rendered to the man who is king, because he is king, not because he is a king, not because he is a man; for it is the highest fear and honour due to any mortal man, which is doe to the king, as king.

11. The man and the inferior judge are different; and we cannot, by this text, resist the inferior judge, as a judge, but we resist the ordinance of God, as the text proveth. But cavaliers resist the inferior judges as men, and have killed divers members of both houses of parliament; but they will not say that they killed

them as judges, but as rebels. If, therefore, to be a rebel, as a wicked man, and to be a judge, are differenced thus, then to be a man, and commit some acts of tyranny, and to be the supreme judge and king, are two different things.

12. The congregation, in a letter to the nobility, (Knox, Hist. of Scotland, 1.2.) say, "There is great difference betwixt the authority, which is God's ordinance, and the persons of those who are placed in authority. The authority and God's ordinance can never do wrong, for it commandeth that vice and wicked men be punished, and virtue, with virtuous men and just, be maintained; but the corrupt person placed in their authority may offend, and most commonly do contrary to this authority. And is then the corruption of man to be followed, by reason that it is clothed with the name of authority?" And they give instance in Pharaoh and Saul, who were lawful kings and yet corrupt men. And certainly the man and divine authority differ, as the subject and the accident,-as that which is under a law and can offend God, and that which is neither capable of law nor sin.

It is true, so long as kings remain kings, subjection is due to them because kings; but that is not the question. The question is, if subjection be due to them, when they use their power unlawfully and tyrannically. Whatever David did, though he was a king, he did it not as king; he deflowered not Bathsheba as king, and Bathsheba might with bodily resistance and violence lawfully have resisted king David, though kingly power remained in him, while he should thus attempt to commit adultery; else David might have said to Bathsheba, "Because I am the Lord's anointed, it is rebellion in thee, a subject to oppose any bodily violence to my act of forcing of thee; it is unlawful to thee to cry for help, for if any shall offer violently to rescue thee from me, he resisteth the ordinance of God." Subjection is due to Nero as an emperor, but not any subjection is due to him in the burning of Rome, and torturing of Christians, except you say that Nero's power abused in these acts of cruelty was, 1. A power from God. 2. An ordinance of God. 3. That in these he was minister of God for the good of the commonwealth.

11

MAGISTRATES' RIGHTS

THEODORE BEZA'S RIGHT OF MAGISTRATES

Source: Julian H. Franklin, translator and ed., *Constitutionalism and Resistance in the Sixteenth Century: Three Treatises by Hotman, Beza, & Mornay,* (A Pegasus Original—original: 1574), 103–05, 112, 124–25, 127, 131–35.

. . . Is there then no remedy at all, it will be asked, against a sovereign who abuses his dominion against all law divine and human? . . . For to put the matter properly, those who teach that notorious tyranny may be resisted in good conscience are not denying good and legitimate rulers the authority that God has given them, nor are they encouraging rebellion. On the contrary, the authority of magistrates cannot be stabilized, nor that public peace, which is the end of all true governance, preserved unless tyranny is prevented from arising or else abolished when it does. The question, then, is to see if there is some means, in accord with justice and the will of God, by which subjects may curb manifest tyranny on the part of a sovereign magistrate, by force of arms if need be. (pp. 103-104)

I admit that prayers united with repentance are proper and necessary remedies to tyranny since it is most often an evil or scourge sent by God for the chastisement of nations. But for all of this, I deny that it is illicit for peoples oppressed by notorious tyranny to make use of lawful remedies in addition to repentance and prayers, and I now present the reasons for my view. (pp. 104–5)

Is it not then reasonable, by all law divine and human, that more should be permitted to these lesser magistrates, in view of their sworn duty to preserve the law, than to purely private persons without office? I say, therefore, that they are obliged, if reduced to that necessity, and by force of arms where that is possible, to offer resistance to flagrant tyranny, and to safeguard those within their care, until such time as the Estates, or whoever holds the legislative power of the kingdom or the empire, may by common deliberation make further and appropriate provision for the public welfare. This, moreover, is not to be seditious or disloyal towards one's sovereign, but to be loyal fully and to keep one's faith toward those from whom one's office was received against him who has broken his oath and oppressed the kingdom he ought to have protected. (p.112)

Let them, therefore, who so exalt the authority of sovereigns as to dare say that no matter what kings do they have no other judge than God, prove to me that there ever was a nation so unmindful of its interests as to submit itself-knowingly and without intimidation or constraint-to the will of a sovereign, without attaching the condition, expressed or implied, that they must be justly and equitably governed. (p. 124)

But suppose that a people-either through foolishness, or blandishments, or because they have had a good prince and presume his offspring will be like him-have submitted to someone absolutely and without express condition. Shall we say that this prince may do anything he pleases, or must we not imply, as if expressed, conditions which are in their nature, holy and in accordance with the law? If not, then how shall we survive, and what will be the life of men, if this prince were to kill his mother and his father, and violate young girls and women, and pillage and massacre subjects at his whim, on the pretest that the people, trusting the probity of that prince, accepted him without condition?

And it would surely be monstrously unfair to deny to an entire nation what equity concedes to private persons such as minors, women, and the simple-minded, as well as to those who have been cheated in a bargain by more than half the just price-especially where the damage to these persons seems to result from the bad faith of the party who is benefited. Is there anyone whose faith is worse than a tyrant so brazen as to claim a right to all things right or wrong because he obtained this right by contract with his people, or received such power from his forebears? (p.125)

But suppose it be objected that public law, which relates to the state of a people or a nation (for it is of this that we are speaking), is different from a law of nature that is common to all peoples. I admit that there are certain differences but hold that these depend on special circumstances, which is not to deny a general and universal rule of equity and rectitude so firm that a government that goes against it-which approves obvious irreligion, robberies, and other things notoriously opposed to God, the law of nature, and good custom-must be repudiated and condemned. (p.127)

VIII. May princes be resisted for unjust taxation?

Suppose we are asked about a prince who oppresses his people with unjust taxes and subsidies. After remonstrations have been made, those having authority may and should restore order according to the laws of the realm, as we have indicated. But this also should be noted: a prince who exceeds his power in a matter like this should not be hastily judged a tyrant simply because he is extravagant, greedy, or given to some other vice. Tyranny implies confirmed wickedness involving general subversion of the political order and of the fundamental laws of a realm. I further say that even where there is just occasion for forcible resistance to tyranny, this important maxim should be kept in mind (even though it was a pagan who enunciated it), namely, that wise men explore things very carefully before they take up arms.

IX. May subjects make agreements with their princes?

I must also answer those who think it wrong for subject to make agreements with a [ruling] sovereign. What are their arguments? If reason is the test, I can think of no sufficient ground. They say that it is for subjects to take orders from the king, not the reverse; that subjects, therefore, may express grievances to their prince with all due reverence and may give their advice when it is asked, but they may not go any further. Subjects, I reply, should surely not approach their supreme or lesser magistrates except with honor and reverence, and not only for fear of provoking them to wrath but for conscience's sake, as the Apostle teaches us, since their position it ordained by God. Yet I deny that the above conclusion necessarily follows from this rule, as if, in matters of public order, after explaining to sovereign, with all reverence, the course of action demanded by reason and by justice and also by the conditions under which he was raised to his position, one must necessarily put up with anything the sovereign may please to do and forego all further remedy. I say, rather, that in this situation it is not unjust to lead him back into the path of duty and even to take stronger measure if reason proves of no avail. (pp. 131-32)

X. May force be used to resist religious persecution?

It remains only to resolve an issue of the greatest consequence. Where there is tyranny in matters of religion, may persecution be resisted by force of arms according to the above distinctions and conditions? The principal objection here is that since religion is a matter of conscience, which may not be coerced, it should not be established by arms. . . .

I answer, to begin with, that it is utterly absurd and false to say that worldly methods of resistance, such as appeal to courts or resort to arms, are not only different from spiritual resistance, but are also so opposed and repugnant to it that they can have no place whatsoever in religious matters. On the contrary, the chief duty of a good magistrate is to employ all the means that God has given him to make sure that God is recognized and served as king of kings by the subjects whom God has committed to his care. To this end, accordingly, he should use the weapon of the law against disturbers of the true religion who will not listen to the admonitions and censures of the Church and his military arm against those who cannot otherwise be halted. (p.133)

I reply that it is one thing to introduce religion in a country, another to preserve it once it is established or to restore it when it has been buried, as it were, under the connivance, ignorance, and wickedness of men. I hold, then, that religion is planted and increased by the Spirit of God alone, through the Word, which is ordained for teaching, encouraging, and exhorting, since this is the special activity of the Holy

Spirit, which works by spiritual means. The duty of a prince who would convert his subjects from idolatry or superstition to true religion is to see that they are given good and lively instruction, while the duty of subjects, correspondingly, is to yield to reason and to truth.

But what may subjects do if there is an attempt to force idolatry upon their conscience? Any effort to force the prince to alter established public order would surely be entirely wrong. They should rather endure persecution patiently while continuing to serve God, or else go into exile. But if there are edicts, lawfully passed and promulgated by public authority, permitting exercise of the true religion, then the prince, I maintain, is even more bound to respect these than any other law since the religious order is of greater consequence than any other, and he may not repeal them at his own initiative and discretion. If he does, he is guilty of flagrant tyranny, to which opposition is permitted according to the distinctions previously laid down, and with all the better reason in that our souls and our consciences ought to be more precious to us than all the goods of this world. (pp. 134–35)

. . . I do not hold that where religion is authorized by law, it must always be defended against open tyranny by force of arms. But that this can be done in good conscience by those with appropriate authority when God has given them the means is attested by the example of Libnah against Jehoram, of Jerusalem against Amaziah, and the war of Constantine against Maxentius at the request of the city of Rome, all of which have been cited. And I thus conclude that we must honor as martyrs not only those who have conquered without resistance, and by patience only, against tyrants who have persecuted the truth, but those also who, authorized by law and by competent authorities, devoted their strength to the defense of true religion. . . . (p. 135)

FURTHER SUGGESTED READING

1) *A Christian Manifesto,* Francis Schaeffer
2) *The Great Christian Revolution*
3) *The Kingship of Christ,* Encyclical Letter of Pope Pius XI
4) *Knox* - Jaspar Ridley
5) *Let Every Man Be Armed: The Evolution of a Constitutional Right,* Stephen P. Halbrook
6) *Political Sermons of the American Founding Era,* ed. Ellis Sandoz
7) *Robespierre, The Fool as Revolutionary: Inside the French Revolution,* Otto Scott
8) *Safeguarding Liberty: The Constitution and Citizen Militias,* ed. Larry Pratt